# MAN MUST EAT

## SIR WILLIAM SLATER

### THE UNIVERSITY OF CHICAGO PRESS

CHICAGO AND LONDON

*Library of Congress Catalog Card Number: 64-13951*

THE UNIVERSITY OF CHICAGO PRESS, CHICAGO & LONDON
The University of Toronto Press, Toronto 5, Canada

# FOREWORD

THE SECTION of Nuclear Medicine in the Department of Pharmacology at the University of Chicago was founded in 1959 with a long-term grant from the Rockefeller Foundation. The name of the section suggests that it is concerned with the use of nuclear energy in medicine. In fact, that is only an indirect part of its work. Its primary activity is the study of the impact and influence of the peaceful applications of nuclear energy upon the health and welfare of mankind. Dr. Lowell T. Coggeshall and Dr. George V. LeRoy of the University of Chicago and Dr. John Bugher, then of the Rockefeller Foundation, recognized that most scientists had directed their energies toward special problems in physics, chemistry, engineering, biology, medicine, and agriculture. It is true that their studies were very frequently of a fundamental, searching nature. In the context of this discussion, however, they were insularly pragmatic in a direct sense. Many scientists had expressed vigorous and various opinions about nuclear energy and its association with military weapons. A lesser number had spoken about the consequences of peaceful uses of nuclear energy, and those who did speak had done so with uncritical voices. These three men, as representatives of the University of Chicago and the Rockfeller Foundation, initiated a program at the University of Chicago that could serve as a center for inquiry, criticism, and public information on the peaceful uses of nuclear energy. The course that that program, soon to be designated the Section of Nuclear Medicine, would follow was easily forecast. The Rockefeller Foundation for a long time has supported programs in medicine and agriculture over the world which have had great social and economic importance. The University of Chicago Faculty of Medicine has

shown a similar interest in medicine. The man selected to head
the Section of Nuclear Medicine was trained in veterinary medicine, a discipline that reaches into both medicine and agriculture;
it was inevitable that the activities of the newly formed section
would touch on both these fields.

Some might question whether medicine and agriculture have
much in common in the discussions that have developed, but
such a view is extremely short-sighted and clearly unfounded.
It is only necessary to recognize that many if not most of the
hazards from the peaceful uses of nuclear energy will reach man
through his food supply. This most certainly brings medicine
and agriculture together in searching for a solution. Even more
important, though, is the hard fact that saving lives and improving health through medical practice are only meaningful if
agriculture can keep pace and supply the food needed to maintain the life and health of those saved. Medical and agricultural
sciences, because of their interdependence, must increasingly
work as a team if they are to serve mankind fully.

In any cold analysis of the recent advances and developments
in the medical and agricultural sciences, it is quite apparent that
medicine leads. However, there are areas in which agriculturists
have a definite advantage. One might mention that biological
statistics was an early achievement of agricultural investigators,
and agricultural research remains today the source of many of
the best contributions to the discipline of statistics on which
medical investigators must depend. It is a better evaluation of
the state of the two sciences to say that medical science, in its
artful practice, is applicable to a wide variety of conditions
throughout the world, while agricultural science in its artful
practice tends to be more regional and national in its application.
It is unfortunate that agricultural science has had its least impact
in those nations and regions where it is most needed. In these
same nations and regions, medical science has made a comparatively more substantial contribution. Many lives have been
saved and many more mouths are searching for food, but food

is not always available for these mouths. It is here that the agricultural scientist can play his great role in the grim drama of mankind's fight for survival. He can, if successful, materially reduce social unrest by reducing hunger. His role deserves equal billing with that of the medical scientist. Both participants must recognize the need each has for the other, and when one falters the other must help him regain his stride. If together they can help to heal the sick and to feed the hungry, they will be working toward a more peaceful and contented mankind.

The author of this book, Sir William Slater, was invited by the University of Chicago to deliver four public lectures on nuclear science and agriculture. He has augmented those lectures for publication. By his personal and scientific experience Sir William long ago qualified himself to speak upon the subject. He has for many years been concerned with the social and economic importance of agriculture throughout the world. Sir William was secretary of the Agricultural Research Council for the United Kingdom during the critical post–World War II years when the United Kingdom was changing its agricultural policy from one of free trade, with a major dependence upon the importation of foodstuffs, to a policy by which it produced a substantial proportion of the agricultural foods needed within the British Isles. Lord Rothschild was chairman of the Agricultural Research Council during this period, and these two men formed an especially effective team. They developed a strong research program in British agriculture which is the envy of all scientific agriculturists. Their joint contribution to the recent transformation of British agriculture cannot be measured, but it must be substantial.

Sir William was a key person in the acceptance and development of radioactive tracer techniques by agricultural investigators. He has also played an important part in the establishment of laboratories in the United Kingdom for measurement and assessment of the hazards from radioactive fall-out in food crops and livestock. From the beginning of these programs he believed that a close liaison should be maintained with the United States and any other nations similarly interested in agricultural research and radioactive fall-out. As a consequence, he was asked to serve as chairman of two important working committees of the Food and Agricultural Organization of the United Nations set up to study and report upon these problems, and he has developed a broad understanding at the international level. Sir William has always demonstrated an awareness of the social and economic importance of agriculture, and since his retirement from the Agricultural Research Council he has addressed himself to this interest. He has also been active in fostering the agricultural developments of the newly emerging nations.

It is not just a coincidence that Lady Slater, his wife, who is also scientifically trained, has taken a great interest in the work of improving the lot of women in these same nations. Both Sir William and Lady Slater were chemistry students at the University of Manchester in the second decade of the century, and both were strongly influenced by the many great men who were their teachers and associates there at that time.

When Sir William was first asked to speak on nuclear science and agriculture at the University of Chicago, he quickly pointed out that to talk only on nuclear science as it is related to agriculture would not be enough. It would be better, he believed, to consider the historical development of research in agriculture and to place the use of nuclear science in agricultural research in correct perspective; and this is what he has done. As one studies this material, one realizes that nuclear science has had few direct applications in agriculture, compared with many in medicine. Research workers in agriculture have, however, made increasing use of radio-isotope techniques in the solution of many of their problems. These techniques are destined to play an ever increasing part in agricultural research, and it is to be hoped that the service they render will do much to counterbalance the anxieties created by the coming of nuclear science.

In Chapter IV, on the less developed nations, Sir William is not particularly optimistic about the assistance that nuclear science can give to their agriculture. Before the sophisticated procedures of nuclear technology can be of use in these countries, such problems must be solved as the economic disturbance caused by intense political nationalism and the social rejection of the farmer, and of the agricultural scientist who works with his hands, by the newly urbanized citizens. The solving of such problems can greatly accelerate the growth of the agricultural economy in new nations and contribute to their strength and stability, for it is rare that a nation can achieve economic stability without a sound agriculture.

As moderators we were fortunate to have Dr. Joseph Ackerman, head of the Farm Foundation, for Sir William Slater's lecture on "Farms and Farmers"; Dr. Emil Mrak, chancellor of the University of California at Davis, for the lecture on "Food and Food Processing"; Dr. D. Gale Johnson, dean of the Division of the Social Sciences at the University of Chicago, for the lecture on "The Developing Nations"; and Dr. Cyril L. Comar, head of the Department of Physical Biology at Cornell University, for the lecture on "Fall-out and Food Chains." They added their own personal observations and encouraged questions from the audience. We have chosen not to include these comments or the questions raised by the audience, except in the case of Dr. Comar, who spoke on the special problems of fall-out for the United States, which in several respects are different from those for the United Kingdom.

We wish to thank all of these men for their assistance. In addition, our thanks are due to Mr. Talmadge Gornto of the University of Chicago Extension Division, whose work in developing the program was so valuable, and to Dr. John T. Wilson, special assistant to President George W. Beadle of the University of Chicago, whose wise counsel was frequently sought.

JOHN H. RUST
Professor of Pharmacology
Head, Section of Nuclear Medicine
The University of Chicago

# CONTENTS

# CONTENTS

# 1

# INTRODUCTION

**T**HE FOUR LECTURES which form chapters 2–5 of this book deal with the ways in which the discoveries of nuclear science have affected the production, preservation, and processing of food, together with the part they may play in the growth of the less developed countries and the degree to which their use in nuclear explosions may have contaminated the food of man and animals.

Early in the preparation of the lectures it became evident that, to assess the importance of the part nuclear science could play in increasing and bettering the world's food supplies, it would be necessary to examine the changes it has already brought about and those it may effect in the future, against the historical background of scientific and technological achievements and failures. It was impossible to do this without becoming acutely aware that the lectures formed part of a much wider subject, the study of which is far more important to mankind than any other. This is man's relationship to his environment, to the air he breathes, to the water he drinks, to the land on which he grows his crops, and most of all to the plant and animal life with which he competes for these essential needs. Not only is man competing against other species, but he is also competing against his fellow men.

The high standard of living in more advanced countries has

**1**

tended to mask this basic characteristic in man. Where the competition is only for our secondary needs, it can be cruel enough; but where men are struggling for their primary needs, it is a matter of life and death. It is this fight for a larger share of the world's natural resources, of its available food, and of markets to which its surpluses can be sold, this effort to improve the standard of living at the expense of other competing groups, which is at the base of all wars and revolutions. We may state these struggles in terms of ideologies, but if we examine these ideologies we shall find that they are merely sophisticated expressions of the fundamental characteristic of all living things, the urge first to survive and then to better the conditions of life. Man can rise above this primitive urge. He is capable of altruism and self-sacrifice, of denying himself to provide for others; but many acts of apparent generosity arise from an underlying fear born of his desire to placate his less fortunate brothers or to score in prestige over his immediate rivals. When man is in competition with other species, self-sacrificing generosity finds a strictly limited place. If he is under no great pressure to survive, he may overlook the depredations of his crops and barns by other forms of life. But even here he is greatly influenced by the appeal other creatures make to his aesthetic sense. He will feed birds in winter, though they may ravage his summer crops, because he finds them beautiful and appealing; but he will kill rats without compunction because their appearance is repulsive to him. However, when man is in serious need of food for himself, he can be ruthless. All that can then save the competitors for his food are religious scruples or superstitious prejudices.

The more prosperous, well-fed, and urban the community in which man lives, the further he thrusts all recognition of this competition with other species to the back of his mind. He has learned to expect his food to be available, whenever he wants it, in the local shop or supermarket. His only anxiety is that he have the necessary money to buy it. In this he recognizes competition with his fellow men, but he leaves to the farmer the task of fighting the legion of other claimants for the right to survive. It is only when he receives a mental jolt that he thinks of a loaf of bread in terms of a field of wheat or a beefsteak in relation to a herd of grazing cattle. Even then he may know little of the dangers from which crops and stock must be ruthlessly protected.

The townsman spoils his pets, feeds the birds, and subscribes to societies for the prevention of cruelty to animals, and in doing so imagines that he is living in harmony with all living things. Even the hunter thinks of what he is doing as sport and not as an expression of the primitive instinct to survive by killing for food or by protecting himself from danger.

This struggle for survival results in what is known as the balance of nature. This phrase is misleading in that the word "balance" suggests a static condition, one that has been reached and will remain undisturbed, whereas the relationship between plants and animals is a fluctuating one.

The factors which affect the balance vary greatly in their time and manner of influence. There are those which disturb the balance over short periods of a few years or even from year to year. These changes are nearly all reversible. The most rapid are confined to quickly breeding species, such as fungi, bacteria, and insects, where there may be many generations within a single season. One in which the meteorological conditions favor the multiplication of a pest or disease of crop or stock may result in a serious epidemic. Unless man takes a hand in control, a temporary upset in the balance of nature will result. If there is a succession of years favorable to the pest, the disturbance in the balance may assume major proportions. Fortunately, a succession of equally unfavorable years can restore the original balance.

These short-term reversible changes assume major importance only when they produce secondary effects which either are permanent or require centuries for their readjustment. Thus, a pest attacking a forest may kill a number of trees and create a fire hazard. Lightning may start a fire and a large section of the forest may be destroyed. The natural regeneration which follows will favor the trees whose seeds are helped to germinate by heat, and a new forest will grow up with its own associated flora and fauna.

Most changes of this order, taking place over centuries, do not depend, however, on a short-term disturbance of balance to set them in motion. They arise more often from climatic or geophysical changes or from evolutionary changes in a plant or animal species. Slow, protracted climatic variations result, over centuries, in major shifts in the balance of nature. Receding polar ice caps and shrinking glaciers allow plants and animals to extend their habitat to new areas, where they come into contact with the previously balanced populations with which they compete until a new balance has been struck.

Geophysical changes, while they are often sudden in their effect, take place only after long periods of slow preparatory change. A section of coastline, which has been pounded by the sea for years, gives way at last before a high tide and a gale to turn the land vegetation, with its associated animal population, into a salt marsh with completely different flora and fauna. Or a river after years of erosion bursts through its banks to find a new course to the sea, turning its old valley into a desert and transforming the new one into fertile land. Such changes are rarely reversible and ultimately lead to a new balance of nature. Often these geophysical changes are local in character, but they may affect wide adjacent areas owing to the spread of their new populations. Where they assume major proportions, as when they involve the breaking of a bridge between two land masses, the result over a long period may be two largely different populations.

It is evolutionary changes, however, which have the most profound effect on the balance of nature. They are slow and continuous. As one species becomes more fully adapted to its environment it develops a higher rate of survival while retaining its rate of reproduction, and so increases in numbers at the expense of its less well-adapted competitors.

The evolution of man from his primitive ancestors was at first slow; not until his superior intellect began to develop did it differ from that of other animals. He began to use speech as a means of communication, which enabled him to hand on detailed knowledge from generation to generation. He developed tools to increase his efficiency and weapons for protection and the killing of animals for food and clothing. With these advantages, his chances of survival increased. Without them, he would have been hard put to it to maintain his numbers, ill-equipped as he was with any natural weapons. Even with his power of speech, his tools, and his weapons, he did not increase greatly in numbers up to the beginning of the Christian era. He was still in continuous danger from famine, wild animals, and the ravages of disease. Man's reproductive rate was low compared with many other mammals; the female rarely bore more than one child in a year. If the conditions which still obtain in many primitive tribes can be taken as a guide, the average period of childbearing was not more than ten or twelve years and infant mortality was eight or nine of each ten births. The average life of the male was probably no longer than that of the female, so that the children raised to maturity no more than maintained the population.

In the last two thousand years man has improved his weapons and has increasingly moved into large centers of population. He has slowly exterminated or driven into the wilder parts of the country the animals he feared. The bear became extinct in England in the eleventh century and the wolf three hundred years later. Now there is no large animal in Britain which man has to fear either for himself or his domestic animals, except perhaps the fox raiding the chicken run; and it, too, would have been destroyed were it not protected for sport.

The movement into larger centers of population brought its own dangers in the form of epidemic diseases due to overcrowding, poor water supplies, and bad sanitation. It also increased the dangers of malnutrition as people moved farther from the farms producing their food. The freedom which had been won from the dangers of wild animals and famine was at least partially replaced by the greater danger from micro-organisms and an increasingly unbalanced diet. As man later found means to travel more widely, the danger from the spread of disease increased, and wars changed from tribal encounters to large-scale conflicts between nations.

All these factors tended to keep the human population in check, so that up to the beginning of the nineteenth century there was no great increase in man's numbers. Then, however, the picture began to change, slowly at first, but faster each decade. Man was finding means to conquer the conditions which shortened his life and limited his numbers. This was something entirely new in evolutionary development. No longer was it necessary to wait for the slow process of evolution to adapt the animal to its environment. Now man, without any material change in his genetic makeup, was controlling and changing his environment to make it fit his special needs. The chance emergence of a genetic structure more suited to the existing environment and its subsequent multiplication, which in a slow-breeding animal like man would take hundreds of years, was replaced by changes in the environment to fit the existing population; these could be very rapid and lead immediately to an increase in the survival rate. If, at the same time, the rate of reproduction remained constant at one birth each year for every female, the human population must inevitably rise rapidly.

If, for example, of the children born to each female, not two but four out of ten survive, the population must double in each generation, if we ignore unmated and barren females. It has been in the survival of the young and in the numbers reaching puberty that the control of environment has been most effective and where it differs most from the results of evolution. Genetic changes which fit an animal to its environment are, on the whole, likely to be concerned with its power to hunt or to fight, with its resistance to heat and cold, with its ability to withstand hunger or thirst. Small evolutional changes in these characteristics can affect the survival of the young only to a limited extent, and at best only slowly. Where man controls the environment to meet his own needs, he can and does make changes which profoundly affect infant mortality. Almost everything he does to increase the adult life span affects even more the chance of survival of the child.

The techniques which man has already used to control his environment are many; new techniques are continually being made available by the scientist, and the old improved. Each area of the world, however small or backward, is applying some means of increasing survival. There is, however, a great gulf between those nations with a high standard of living, where every known technique is employed to some extent, and those poor in wealth and education where only the fringes of the problem have so far been touched.

The oldest and in many ways the most important techniques were those in agriculture which led to an adequate food supply. Much later came the knowledge required to select a balanced diet from the food available. Later, too, came many of the means for protecting crops during storage and for preserving surpluses against hungry times. Given the means and the knowledge necessary to provide himself with an adequate diet throughout the year, man, by overcoming hunger and malnutrition, took the first important step in controlling his environment and prolonging his life expectancy.

However important a full and balanced diet may be to the male adult, it is far more so to the lactating mother and to the child immediately after weaning. While a mother is nursing her child, she provides a balanced diet in her milk at the expense of her own body. Unless her diet is so deficient that her milk supply fails, the child will not suffer. What is impaired is her own chance of survival and her ability to continue to bear children. The old saying, "For each child a tooth," applies to many of her body tissues.

When the child is weaned the danger of malnutrition is great. Only when an adequate and safe supply of cow's or other similar milk was available did young children begin to come safely through this difficult period. Before such a source of protein, minerals, and vitamins was available, a child died of malnutrition or from a disease which his undernourished body could not resist, or he survived to carry into adult life weaknesses due to his childhood deprivations.

Another important advance was the control of man's actual physical environment. Extremes of cold and heat can of themselves cause death, particularly in the very young and very old, but the less severe conditions more frequently encountered have a greater effect upon survival rate through their power to weaken resistance to disease. The development of better housing and of means of heating and ventilation have protected all age groups in the population. It is, however, the effects on the young and the old which are most marked. More of the young survive to reproduce their kind, while the old live on to increase further the average life span.

During the nineteenth century the simple tools powered by hand, by domestic animals, or by water were transformed by steam power; they became machines which, as time passed, removed more and more of the physical labor from work. With the twentieth century came the internal combustion engine and the widespread use of electrical power. Now almost every task is lightened by the use of machines. The greatest advances in the present century have been in three major types of work: those on the farm, in civil engineering, and in the home. The tractor and the many other agricultural machines have taken much of the heavy physical work from farming and have enabled fewer men to produce more food. No longer are big civil engineering projects largely a matter of pick, shovel, and wheelbarrow; now they are carried out quickly by massive earth-moving equipment. The housewife has at her disposal an ever-widening range of labor-saving devices to make her tasks physically easier.

The first effect of the wide use of mechanical power on man's ability to survive was not entirely good. It resulted in the crowding together of workers in factories under conditions which favored the spread of diseases. Young children worked long hours in mines and factories, with disastrous effects on their health. It did, however, produce the wealth necessary to buy better food, housing, and clothing. Men were less worn out with sheer physical effort and exposure to the elements.

As man learned to avoid the serious errors which marred the early years of the industrial revolution, the beneficial effect of ample power supplies grew, until now there is no doubt about their contribution to increased length of life. The survival of the young child is not so directly affected as it is by a well-balanced diet or protection from extremes of climate. Indirectly, however, it is profoundly affected by the higher standard of living achieved by its parents, which enables them to provide food and other necessities for a full and healthy life.

It is, however, the advances in medicine and in the related public health services which have had the greatest effect on man's expectation of life. Knowledge of the part micro-organisms play in so many forms of human illness and how the dangers from these unseen invaders of the body can be lessened and controlled has had more influence on survival than any other product of human intelligence. If to the direct consequences of this knowledge are added the advances in surgery which it made possible and the developments in anesthesia which it stimulated, the final effect on man's place in nature is so great that from the time of Pasteur a new epoch in the history of the world began. Nothing that went before can compare with what has followed these great advances in medical science. Disease after disease has been controlled by the use of vaccines and chemotherapy. The spread of infection has been minimized by the treatment of sewage, by the provision of safe water supplies, and by the proper handling of food. The study of insect-borne diseases such as malaria has resulted in their elimination from large areas of the world. The dangers of childbirth have been greatly reduced and, hence, the period during which the female remains capable of reproduction has been lengthened. Surgery has found means of dealing with many conditions which would otherwise terminate life.

As these dangers were removed, the importance of metabolic diseases became increasingly apparent and the value of the study of physiology and biochemistry emphasized. This initiated a chain of investigations which may in the end prove as important as those in microbiology. The results are already having a major effect on human health.

The provision of a correctly balanced diet, made possible by improved food production and processing, depends on the findings of the biochemists. The control of diseases such as diabetes and kwashiorkor and the explanation of malfunctions of organs like the liver and kidneys are being supplied by the joint efforts of clinicians, the physiologists, and biochemists.

No way in which man has adjusted his environment to meet his needs has had so great an effect on the survival of the young as medicine. There seems no reason why the average woman should not, given ample food, good housing and clothing, and all the aids of medicine, produce and rear to puberty not two children but ten or more. The effect of such a reproduction rate would be catastrophic; the human population would increase fivefold or more in a generation and there would be world-wide famine.

That there has been no such violent explosion of population is due to many factors. It is essential we bear in mind the possibility that this rate may be achieved, at least in part. We must study also the factors which have so far held it within bounds. It is only by such studies that future population trends and the world's food requirements can be assessed.

Man's power to control his environment has so far been applied only to a limited extent. The growth of science on which this power rests was in the first place confined to Western Europe, and it was here that the first rapid growth of population took place. That of Britain increased some three and a half times in the nineteenth century, and it is estimated that it will have doubled again by 1970. This is not a high rate of increase; it implies no more than that for each ten females in one generation there should be between twelve and thirteen in the next. The increase is sufficiently alarming, however, resulting as it does in the doubling of the population in less than four generations.

During the first half of the nineteenth century, science had relatively little impact on man's survival rate. It was only during the second half that the mass of people in Britain was able to purchase food in both quantity and variety sufficient to provide a reasonably adequate diet. There was still serious malnutrition, due partly to lack of knowledge of what constituted a balanced diet and partly to the inability of the lowest wage-earners to buy enough of the more expensive foods with special nutritive qualities, such as milk.

Housing, too, was improving slowly in Britain. Workers' cottages in the towns were at least weatherproof and warmed with fires of coal from the pits. A potable supply of running water was generally available, but sanitation was still primitive. Except among the very poor there was enough clothing of a kind to keep out the cold and the damp, but children could be seen barefoot and in rags at the beginning of the twentieth century.

Although medical knowledge was advancing rapidly, its impact on population growth was still relatively small. Childbirth was dangerous both for mother and child. The only vaccine in general use was that against smallpox. If the mother's milk failed, the child was in serious danger from malnutrition and from infected milk.

Diseases from which the modern child is protected by vaccines, or which can be rendered virtually harmless by modern drugs and treatment, were even in the early years of the present century the cause of heavy child mortality. The simplest surgical techniques were often fatal. Anesthetics were limited to chloroform and ether and antiseptics to strong corrosive substances, of which carbolic acid was by far the most used. Tuberculosis was common and nearly always fatal and pneumonia was often fatal in the young and strong and meant almost certain death to the middle-aged and old.

The last half of the nineteenth century was one in which women bore many children. If the survival rate had approached that now achieved in Britain, the population would have more than doubled in each generation. That it did not increase at this rate was due primarily to the high mortality among children and to a lesser degree to early deaths among the adult population. Another contributory factor was the emigration of large numbers of the young and strong to the newly developing countries in America and Australasia.

From the time of World War I the position in Britain has been reversed. Infant mortality has been falling quickly; deaths among young children, once so common, are now rare. Since World War II malnutrition in children is almost unknown and in adults is due more often to overeating than to privation. Housing, sanitation, and water supplies are reaching new standards, although there is still much to be done. The killing diseases of the young, such as tuberculosis, pneumonia, and diabetes, are no longer feared. Surgery in all its forms has become increasingly safe. It is true that many diseases have yet to be conquered, but the chance that a pregnancy will add another unit to the population and leave the mother fit and able to bear more children has increased greatly.

Yet the population has been rising at a somewhat slower rate than in the nineteenth century. There can be only one way in which this can have come about: each female must have had fewer pregnancies. In other words, the reproduction rate has been controlled. With reasonable certainty that the children born will survive and grow to manhood and womanhood, parents have planned their families. They have decided how many children they can bring up in the standard of living they have come to accept, and have limited the pregnancies to this number.

For this kind of family planning to take place on a nationwide scale, certain conditions are essential. The most important is an educational system which insures a literate population capable of understanding what is involved in and the advantages which spring from a limited family. A secondary effect of such an educational system is that so long as children are in school they do not contribute to the family income, but instead make demands on it. In modern Britain, children are no longer considered a financial asset as they were when they went to work at a tender age.

A second condition required to bring about family planning is a high and rising standard of living for the population as a whole. Higher nutritional standards increase the expense of feeding each child. Better housing means that overcrowding cannot be accepted; a large family now means a larger house. No longer can children go about in rags; they must be properly dressed when they attend school. As a result, each additional child makes a demand on the family income, for which it must compete with the amenities the parents may desire not only for themselves but for their other children.

The means of restricting pregnancies are controversial. In Britain contraceptive measures are widely accepted and practiced

and are largely responsible for the reduction in the rate of reproduction. We see, therefore, in Britain, that a rough balance has
been struck between the rates of survival and reproduction which
has resulted in a twofold increase in population in a little under
four generations, if we assume twenty years to a generation. If
the present rate of increase in population continues (and there
is no evidence that it is slackening; it rather is tending to rise), the
population of Britain will reach somewhere over 70,000,000 by
the end of the century. If the present standard of feeding is to be
maintained, this population will need about 40 per cent more food
than is now consumed.

British farming provides little more than half of the country's
food requirements; the rest is imported. Although the average
yield per acre of cultivable land is already one of the highest in
the world, it can be raised still further if the poorest farmers can
be brought up to the level of the better. It is difficult, however, to
see how it could be raised by more than the 40 per cent which
would be necessary to maintain the present proportion of home-
grown food. There is little more land suitable for farming, and
what there is must be eroded to provide living space for the increased population. In order to feed her people, Britain will have
to increase her imports of food at least in proportion to the increase in her population.

In most of the Western European countries, in North America,
and in Australasia the number of pregnancies resulting in the
addition of an adult member to the population has been following
the same pattern as in Britain. At the same time there has been
a similar development of family planning by limitation of the
number of pregnancies. The incidence of the increased survival
rate and of voluntary family limitation has varied from country
to country, with a corresponding effect on the rise in population.
There have also been large movements by emigration from the
heavily populated countries of Western Europe to North America, Australasia, and South Africa.

The general result, in all the more developed countries, is a balance between an increasing survival rate and a limitation of reproduction which has resulted in a steady increase in population of the same order as that in Britain during the last half-century. As yet, this has not led to a food shortage in these countries. In Britain home production cannot meet the demand, but there has always been money to buy surpluses from other countries. In other countries, in particular the United States and Canada, there are at present embarrassing surpluses. Their growing populations will, however, gradually absorb these surpluses; thus it is estimated that with the present level of production the people of the United States will be consuming all the food they produce by 1970. There will be an ample reserve for the people of the United States in the additional potential output from their land, but it is doubtful whether there will be from then on a surplus for export.

In the less developed countries of the world, the impact of science has come much later and in different forms. Whereas in the older countries universal education and industrial progress, resulting in a higher standard of living, were taking place side by side with advances in medicine, in the younger countries modern medicine has begun to affect the rate of survival among peoples still largely illiterate, without industrial wealth, and with a low standard of living. Therefore those factors which in older countries resulted in limitation of pregnancies are largely absent, while medicine is reducing infant mortality and increasing expectation of adult life.

The two major gifts which colonial governments brought to the countries they ruled were medical knowledge and a stable government. The latter reduced internecine wars and began to put an end to infanticide and to human sacrifice. The former began the almost impossible tasks of helping millions of suffering humanity and of caring for mothers and young children. Everything that was done was calculated to take the existing brakes off population growth. In many countries, infanticide, particularly of females, was a primitive form of family limitation. There may, too, have been a vague consciousness that war and human sacrifice were essential if the number of mouths to be fed was not to exceed the available food. The death of many young children was accepted as inevitable, and suffering from disease was regarded as part of life. The task of the colonial administrators was enormous. Progress was at first slow, but since the beginning of the century the effects have been shown in an increasing rate of population growth. The colonial powers attempted to match the growing population by improving primitive agriculture, but doing so is more difficult than providing medical services. Much medical knowledge gained in the older countries could be applied directly in the colonial territories. Where the diseases to be cured were peculiar to these countries, they could be attacked on the basis of fundamental knowledge accumulated in the laboratories of the old countries. Moreover, each problem was essentially simple; the objective was to cure the disease without any economic considerations other than the provision of funds for research and treatment.

Agriculture presented a much more complicated task. Most of the colonial territories were in the tropics and subtropics, with conditions of soil and climate not known in the older countries, situated as they are in the temperate zones. Few of the crops which form the basis of the agriculture of Western Europe were suitable to the tropics, and almost none of traditional methods of cultivation. Men had to be specially trained for this work. When they reached the countries to which they were assigned they had to study the existing farming methods, the soil, and the climate and introduce new methods with the greatest caution. A serious mistake resulting in a crop failure meant a loss of confidence which took years of work to restore. Effort had to be divided between food production and cash crops which provided the farmers with money to spend and the territory with export earnings. Apart from plantations of cash crops managed largely by Europeans, there was a multiplicity of small farms producing food; the men farming them were unable to read and could be reached only by personal visits to each holding or at least to each village. There was no center such as a hospital or clinic to which the farmers could come for help. Moreover, the agriculturalist had always to keep in mind problems of transport and marketing, once he had succeeded in getting the farmers to grow food in excess of their own requirements. Before he recommended better tools, better seeds, or the use of fertilizers, he had to make certain the farmer could afford them, that they were available, and that the final return would justify the expenditure. He had to battle administrators to get the necessary funds to start a better system of production, to get roads built to carry away produce and to bring in supplies, or to get the necessary regulations passed for the control of pests and diseases. Perhaps most difficult of all, he had to fight tradition and prejudice, always with a half-fear that there might after all be wisdom in the local farming folklore.

It is not to be wondered that food production in many territories fought a losing battle against population growth. Overcropping and overstocking increased as the pressure on land grew. Years of continuous cultivation without any adequate return in dung or other fertilizer exhausted the soil in many parts of the world, so that without added nutrients the yields were pitiably low. Herds of largely unproductive cattle overgrazed what pasture was available and so further reduced their value as food producers.

Since World War II one colonial territory after another has achieved independence. As a result, many Europeans working in the territories have left and been replaced by nationals of the new countries. A large proportion of the students from these ex-colonial territories trained overseas have studied to become administrators, lawyers, and doctors; few have elected to train in agriculture. The health services have thus tended to suffer less from the staff changes than have the other technical services. This disparity has served further to emphasize the differing rates of progress in medicine and agriculture.

Independence has given a great impetus to the development of the new nations. Not only the ex-colonial powers but many other nations, in particular the United States, have made large sums available in aid. Plans have been made for education, for the exploitation of natural resources, for the provision of power, for the extension of transport systems, for industrialization, and for the improvement of agriculture. But with all the help that can be given in men and money, the task is so great that progress can only be slow. Education depends on the training of teachers and the building and equipping of schools; the exploitation of natural resources calls for geologists and cartographers; the provision of power and the extension of transport require civil and mechanical engineers; industrialization cannot proceed without expert technicians of many different kinds; and agriculture needs research and advisory officers trained in this and in the many other sciences which serve the farmer. Such men are not available in sufficient numbers either in the countries themselves or on short-term contracts from the older countries.

There are in these newly independent countries three main factors affecting the relationship between population and available food supplies the expanding health services which affect the survival rate; the growth of literacy and the efforts to raise the standard of living which could, if the pattern of the older countries is followed, lead to the voluntary limitation of pregnancies; and the increase in food production.

All present indications are that the survival rate in the less developed countries is rising rapidly and will continue to do so, that so far efforts to improve education and to raise the standard of living have had little or no effect on the limitation of pregnancies, and that they are likely to do so only slowly.

The disparity between the rate of change in these two factors, survival and reproductive rate, must result in a continuous increase in the speed at which the population of the less developed countries grows, and they are already growing at three to four times that of Europe. In many of these countries there is already hunger; in many more there is serious malnutrition. To maintain this already insufficient food supply for a rapidly growing population will require a great effort to increase food supplies by 20 to 30 per cent in each decade.

How far is this possible, and what does it involve? Various aspects of these questions are examined in the following chapters. It is sufficient to say here that it may be possible for food supplies to keep up with the rise in population, to a ceiling of about eight billion, a figure which will be reached in the twenty-first century. Long before that state is reached, there will have to be many great changes in the world's economic and social organization, in the food habits of nations, and in the methods of food production.

The population pressure, already unequal, will become increasingly so. It will be greatest where there is already hunger and malnutrition, and it is here that a ceiling will be reached long before it is world-wide. Either the people of these countries will have to emigrate to lands where agricultural production can still supply more than enough food for the existing population, or the excess food from other areas will have to be shipped to where there is threat of famine. This is a political and economic problem which will strain relationships between nations. In general, the overpopulated countries are poor and will not be able to pay for the food they will need, nor will countries capable of producing the required food welcome a great influx of migrants from the famine areas.

To produce the additional food there will have to be a world-wide intensification of agriculture, which will inevitably increase the cost in men and materials, including power. Great schemes of irrigation and an enormous increase in the use of fertilizers will be required. Changes in diet will be called for, not only in the famine areas but also in those still adequately supplied with food.

The famine areas will have to adapt themselves to foodstuffs which can best be produced under other climatic conditions. The supplying countries will, in turn, have to adopt more economical uses of farm produce if they are to provide food for export. The present high level of animal protein in the diets of countries with a high standard of living is produced at the expense of many times the energy value in crops on which the stock is fed. High-quality animal protein or its equivalent is essential to a balanced diet, but in many countries twice as much of this protein is eaten as the recommended level of 33 gm. per day. Its consumption can be cut without any danger to health, but at the expense of much gastronomic pleasure.

The opposition which will arise in the wealthier countries to expenditure on the intensive production of food which will either have to be given away or sold at a loss, while the diet of their own people is restricted, will be all the stronger if the countries to be helped refuse for religious or other reasons to help themselves as they should. These political and economic problems will have to be faced well before the end of the century; they will present great difficulties. Already the newly independent nations in Asia and Africa have come to look on aid from the countries of Europe, North America, and Australasia as almost a right. They feel that the wealthier countries have a moral obligation to help them with their problems; the ex-colonial powers because they have benefited from the old relationship, and the other nations because they are in possession of so large a share of the earth's fertile land. Rich and poor alike have many lessons to learn before a stable world situation can be reached. This educational process has already begun, but it is so far largely confined to scientists and medical men. They are beginning to know and understand each other's problems, partly because they have trained and worked together and partly because they see the problem in its factual simplicity, freed from all emotional overtones.

Politicians and educators have an outstandingly difficult task. Although they may know and understand the problem themselves, they find it impossible to make unpleasant truths known to the mass of the people other than by slow degrees. Man has become so accustomed to his power to control his environment that he will not readily accept the idea that the point may have been reached when he can no longer do this. Instead he blames those in authority, believing that they could by some means have avoided the dilemma in which he finds himself, without the need for sacrifice. Scientists must buy time for politicians in every way they can, the agricultural scientist by increasing output from the land, the food scientist by protecting and preserving what is produced, and the dietitian by building the best possible diet from what is available.

The scientist in turn will need help from the politician. He will need both moral and material support. Unless the people know that the scientist has the approval of those in power, his task may become impossible. Without money and materials he cannot put into effect his plans for bettering the nutrition of the people.

Given willing co-operation by all those involved, the food supply can be greatly increased, particularly in those countries where it is most needed. The average yields of rice — the grain on which most people depend — in Europe, Australasia, and Japan are well over 4,000 kg. per hectare, while those in Africa and the Far East are only 1,1000 kg. and 1,650 kg. respectively, the latter in spite of the high yields in Japan. Wheat, the second most important grain crop, varies in yield from 1,930 kg. per hectare in Europe to 840 kg. in the Far East and 570 kg. in Africa.

The difference in the production of high-quality animal protein among these areas is almost certainly greater. It is difficult to draw any really reliable statistics from the herds of impoverished animals which are found in parts of Asia and Africa.

If yields in these countries with a low level of agriculture could be raised immediately to those in Europe or Japan, hunger and malnutrition could be banished. Such a sudden rise is, of course, impossible; any change will be slow. It is unlikely that under the most favorable circumstances the agricultural output will do more than keep pace with the growing population and maintain the present low level of nutrition. If it does no more than this, it will provide the time which is sorely needed for those other factors to begin to operate which can diminish the number of pregnancies, the only real solution to the world's population problems.

There is, however, a limit to the time in which agriculture can hold the position. To obtain high yields, it is not only necessary that crops be grown from good seed and be well fertilized, but there must also be an adequate supply of water. In many parts of the world this can be provided only by irrigation. Leaving aside the great cost of irrigation schemes, a cost which tends to rise as land less accessible to water is brought under cultivation, there is a limit to the amount of suitable water available. Calculation as to the amounts must be highly speculative. The problem is different in each area, and we know all too little about the interrelation of supplies. There are often large underground connections between sources, so that drawing large quantities from one may result in the failure of another. What is clear, however, is that water will be one of the factors placing a limit on production — probably the most important. Much can be done to conserve water supplies and to provide additional sources. The use of a thin film of cetyl alcohol to prevent evaporation has been successful over small water surfaces; it fails where the surface is big enough to allow extensive wave formation. The prevention of losses by seepage from canals by suitable linings can bring important savings. Studies of the economical use of irrigation water and of the possibilities of using brackish water are also already increasing the areas which can be irrigated. As population pressure builds up, man himself will become a serious competitor for water. Apart from drinking water, he needs large supplies for sewage disposal and for industry. These may be met in part by saline water and in part by desalination processes. These, however, require power supplies of an order which, at least for the time being, makes their use for irrigation impracticable.

The other major limiting factor, which may prove more important than the water supply, is the land on which crops can be grown. These two factors are interrelated: there may be more land on which crops might be grown than can be irrigated; alternatively, there may in the end prove to be more than enough water to bring all potentially cultivable land into production. Man has many other demands on the earth's land surface which compete with agriculture. The rising population will want more land for housing and for industry. Often the only land suitable for these purposes is that either already producing food or capable of doing so. It will be essential to conserve every acre for agriculture, if a shortage of land is not in the end to bring famine to the world. In the past there has been prodigal waste of good agricultural land in many industrialized countries. It is so often the cheapest to develop, being relatively flat, well drained, and already provided with some roads. In Britain this danger has at last been recognized and an attempt is being made to preserve the agricultural land which remains. It is vitally important that as much agricultural land as possible should be preserved in the newly developing countries where there is a demand for new industries and improved housing.

Agriculture is not the only source of food; the sea and inland waters provide large quantities of valuable food of high protein content. Sea and fresh-water fishing differ from agriculture in that they are essentially forms of hunting wild life. In any activity of this type it is important to control the amount and kind of the catch. With a growing world population the danger is that there will be serious over-fishing, with reduction of the breeding stock. As the sea is fished by many nations, it is vital that there should be agreement on the control of fishing practices. It will, however, be difficult to persuade a hungry nation to keep these rules. Fishing of inland waters within one country can be more easily regulated, but even here hunger may make the policing of laws difficult, if not impossible.

There is a possible additional source of food in the fish of the deeper oceans. This has been inadequately explored and depends on careful investigation to ascertain whether deep-sea fishing will upset the ecological balance to the disadvantage of easier fishing on the continental shelves.

Fish farming in shallow waters, such as paddy fields, can provide a valuable source of food. Ponds can be fertilized to encourage the vegetation on which small fish feed and so achieve a high yield of small fish. In tropical countries, it is claimed that an acre of properly managed fish pond can produce more protein than any crop grown on land. This is undoubtedly a most promising source of food and one which should be exploited wherever the conditions are favorable.

A number of less orthodox sources of food are also being examined. The cells of green parts of plants such as grass contain proteins similar in value to those in foods of animal origin. They are, however, largely inaccessible to animals other than ruminants, because of their inability to digest the cell walls. Attempts have been made with varying success to break the cell walls and so free the protein, which can then be separated and used to feed human beings or animals like pigs and poultry. It is not easy to persuade people to eat these proteins, which are at first unpalatable, unless there is real need. Experiments are being made to try to introduce them into the accepted dishes of countries where there is a serious protein shortage, without materially changing the taste.

This experimental work is of importance because it is providing knowledge which at some future date may save many from serious malnutrition.

Another possible source of food is the use of yeasts or other micro-organisms, which will utilize waxes and other petroleum products as a basis for the synthesis of protein from inorganic nitrogen. This work is in its early stages, but it may prove to be a most valuable source of food which does not make any call on land other than the small area required for the building in which fermentation takes place.

Examination of the relation between man's survival and reproduction rates can lead only to the conclusion that his power to control his environment without any equivalent control of his rate of reproduction will, if these factors continue to operate unchanged, result in a position where his growing numbers are in the end checked by lack of food, over the production of which he has only limited control. In this he will only be repeating what has in the past happened to other species which have outgrown the available food supply.

Man, however, differs from other species in a number of ways. His knowledge of science enables him to exterminate any serious competitors for his food supply. It allows him to increase his food supply far beyond anything that is available in the surrounding wild life. He can preserve, store, and distribute his food over long periods and distances and so overcome the periodic local famines due to crop failure.

The dangers from the rapid increase in world population can be avoided only if the peoples of the world recognize it and are prepared to make the necessary adjustments and sacrifices. It is unfortunate that early warnings against a rising population proved to be too pessimistic because of underestimation of the possible agricultural output. As a result, there is a prevailing feeling that once again warnings will prove to be wrong and that all will still come right in the end, without any personal effort other than some charitable gifts from those with plenty to those in need.

The task of educating public opinion is difficult. No one wishes to be told that he must be prepared to accept changes in his social attitudes and religious beliefs, yet both will be brought into question. Few, if any, will contend that medical aid should not be made increasingly available in the less developed countries, that children should be allowed to die from lack of knowledge of medical care and medicines or from withholding large schemes of disease control. Even if the wealthier nations were callous enough to refrain from giving this help, which in itself is unthinkable, the less developed countries would still progress, although more slowly, through the efforts of their own medical men.

This, then, is the world's dilemma: that having found the means of overcoming early death, it must take steps to prevent the creation of life in excess of that for which food can be provided. Both the limitation of reproduction and the expansion of food production are hedged around with beliefs and prejudices, religious and emotional, which have to be overcome.

No subject is more controversial than the means to be employed to limit the number of births. Many views are held with sincerity and conviction. At one extreme is the view that pregnancy should be limited by the exercise of self-control; at the other, that abortion should be legalized and made freely available. Between these extremes are advocated various forms of contraception and sterilization. The holder of one view cannot dictate to the holder of another; rather, each should examine objectively what he is advocating and what effect its application has had so far in limiting population. No one can honestly support the spread of medical care and at the same time support a system of birth control which is not likely to be effective among peoples of widely differing levels of education and standards of living.

The increase in food production is hedged about almost equally by prejudices and beliefs. In many of the less developed countries, religious beliefs and social customs hamper agricultural progress. Large numbers of unproductive and diseased domestic animals that use grazing badly needed for milk and meat production, and wild animals that are held sacred, limit the food which children sorely need. Primitive agriculture is founded on tradition, some based on sound practical experience but much springing from superstitious beliefs of no validity. To persuade the farmer to give up those of his traditional ways which are bad while encouraging him to retain those which are good, when in his eyes both have equal authority, calls for time and tact. The change to modern farming methods must be slow at best, but without this revolution there is no hope of meeting the needs of the peoples of the poorer countries. It is not only in these countries that emotional prejudice and ignorance can hold up agricultural progress. Many people have an irrational belief that the world can be fed by an agriculture which they believe is in tune with nature. They have in mind an idyllic state before science was applied in agriculture, a state which never existed except in a dream world. They speak of man farming his land in balance with nature, when there were no fertilizers other than dung and rotted vegetation and no protection for crops and stock against pests and disease other than their natural immunity. Men did farm in this way and still do in many parts of the world, but the produce of their farms was (and is) small in quantity and poor in quality. If this were to become the universal method, the world would be faced with famine.

Man's growing numbers are continually and irretrievably changing the balance of nature. To live, he must destroy competitors for his food supply. As he farms more land he must drive further away any wild creatures which had this land as their habitat. He must protect his crops from the ravages of invaders, bird or rodent. He must use every means to feed his crops by irrigation and by fertilizers. He must employ every method developed by science for controlling the wild plants which compete with his crops for water and for plant nutrients, and for destroying the pests and diseases which attack his crops. In doing so he will have to use substances which may be dangerously toxic and which, if he is careless, may cause illness or even loss of life. But the choice is clear: to risk a small danger, or to bring hunger and death from malnutrition to millions.

A world in which man must in time destroy all his competitors in order to feed himself is one in which many would not care to live. It would be a drab world without color or variety, with a monotonous and uninteresting diet. Except in those parts of the earth's land surface that are too inhospitable to produce food, the countryside would be no more than one great farm with carefully protected and highly cultivated fields intersected with the minimum number of great highways needed to get from town to town. There would be no wild animals or birds, no flowers in the hedgerows or uncultivated open spaces. If this is a world we do not wish to bequeath to our children, then we must take action to limit severely the number of births. At the same time we must see to it that nowhere in the world is life so poor and wretched that the people do not understand the danger and have ceased to care for tomorrow provided they have their meager ration of food for today.

# 2

# FARMS AND FARMERS

I T IS MY PURPOSE in this chapter to examine the response of agriculture to the growth of population: first historically, to see how far a general pattern emerges; next, to try to assess the position today; and, finally, to consider what can be done to meet the still greater demands of the future.

Agriculture has so far always responded to the call for food from man's growing numbers. To do so, it has first sought more land for its crops and stock, and where this search has failed it has improved its techniques in order to make better use of existing resources. How long can it continue to do so?

Of the earth's total acreage, roughly 10 per cent is arable, producing mostly human food; 20 per cent is under grass, much of little value; 30 per cent is under forest; and the rest consists of towns, mountains, deserts, and wastes. By the extension of irrigation and various other means, more land is steadily being brought into use. Between 1951 and 1959, 900,000,000 acres were added; but as farmland advances into the less hospitable regions of the earth, so the cost in men, power, and materials of producing a ton of food must rise.

In spite of the large increase in acreage in the last decade, the world population has grown faster. In this period the area of land producing food for each human mouth fell from 3.68

to 3.35 acres, yet food supplies have at least held their own because farming techniques have improved.

Speculations about the future relationship between world population and food production, foretelling world hunger, have often proved wrong, not because the increase in population has been overestimated, (rather the reverse) but because the scientist and the farmer have so far managed to keep pace by increasing food production.

One of the major steps in the evolution of civilized man, a step comparable with the invention of the written word or the controlled use of fire, was man's change from a hunter, living precariously on the animals he could catch and the wild fruits he could gather, to a farmer, enjoying the relative security of his flocks, his cultivated land, and his stored crops. As primitive man, by his higher intelligence and acquired skills, multiplied more quickly than the wildlife around him, this great evolutionary change became inevitable. The small family group could find close at hand all the wild animals and plants they needed to supply their simple wants for food and clothing. As the family group grew in size and became a tribe, the wildlife immediately around its dwelling place was exhausted and the hunters and the gatherers of fruits were forced to range over an ever increasing area. Inevitably, a point was reached when the distances involved became too great to carry back from the hunting grounds all that was needed, and so, equally inevitably, the tribe had to move with the hunters to where food was available; in short, they became nomadic.

The next great advance was the domestication of the ruminants. No longer was man dependent on catching wild animals; instead he moved from one grazing ground to another, driving his flocks and herds before him. This way of life still exists, virtually unchanged, in many parts of the world. Nomads in the Middle East or in the Rift Valley in Central Africa still live as their ancestors did thousands of years ago. It is a way of life which has always been and is increasingly threatened by the civilization which has grown up in the towns and villages of a settled countryside. Modern medicine has to some degree protected the nomad from the ravages of disease, and wise administration from the losses due to inter-tribal warfare, with a resulting rise in population. Flocks and herds too have been increasingly protected from disease, so that more men and animals seek to live on the sparse vegetation which is characterisic of most of the land the nomads inhabit. With this growing pressure the herds must, in time, be forced to return to the grazing grounds before a fresh growth of herbage has been established. In the end the land is eaten bare, ready for the wind and rain to erode away the soil, so the potential grazing area is reduced and the competition for what remains is increased. There is no way in which the nomadic way of life can be helped except by reducing the number of men and animals dependent on it and by this means establishing a grazing rotation with an adequate time lapse between each visitation. This method contributes nothing to the solution of the problem of how to feed the world's explosively expanding population.

There was, however, another way open to primitive man, where the soil was good and rainfall adequate. He could clear a patch of land from the existing vegetation and sow there the seeds of plants that provided food for himself and the animals he had domesticated. In this way, by concentrated planting of selected crops, he was able to supply all his needs from a relatively small area and to live a settled life in a village community, surrounded by his fields, his herds, and his storage barns. Later, as the land immediately suitable for this system of farming became settled, other areas with inadequate rainfall were brought under cultivation by systems of irrigation, many of which involved the great early feats of engineering.

It was on this agrarian system of farming that the civilization of the Western world was built. The peasant farmer, as he became more skilled, produced more food than he himself needed and was able to exchange his surplus for the products of craftsmen in metal, pottery, textiles, and leather. Concentrations of these craftsmen formed centers which became famous for the quality of workmanship and which grew until the local farms could no longer meet their needs and food had to be brought in from outlying villages. With the making of roads and easier transport, these concentrations of craftsmen grew in size to form the first cities of the world. No longer was it possible for a direct exchange to be made of the produce of the farm for that of the workshop; a merchant was needed to buy from one and sell to the other. In the cities, too, scholars had leisure to think and to write and artists to decorate. In each tribe arose men of outstanding ability and physical courage who became the overlords, exacting tribute from peasant, craftsman, and merchant alike. From these overlords in turn came the princes and kings of the world. However large and famous the cities became, however powerful and wealthy the princes, they all rested on the base of a peasant population cultivating small strips of land and tending their flocks and herds. In many parts of Europe the general pattern of farming remains much the same today: small fields carefully tended, largely by hand, yielding on each farm a wide range of crops and animal products. There have, of course, been many improvements in the quality of the plants and animals, in the methods of cultivation, in the use of fertilizers, and in the protection of crops and stock from pests and diseases, but on peasant farms these are adopted only slowly; many can never be fully employed in the small fields of peasant farmers who have little capital and often little knowledge of the scientific principles on which the improvements are based.

In England another major change in the farming pattern took place in the fourteenth century. Travel had created in the ruling classes a desire for the products of other lands. The wines of France, the silks and spices of the East, or the craft products of the Low Countries could be purchased only by money earned from exports. England had, in the wool from her sheep, a product which was highly prized. To obtain more of this valuable export material, many of the small open fields of the peasants were taken over and enclosed to provide the larger units of land required for this early form of specialized farming.

The slow growth of population in Britain had by the time of the Civil War, in the middle of the seventeenth century, begun to outrun the production of food from the land. There were, as always, two ways by which more food could be produced: one, to bring into cultivation more land, and the other, to produce more on the land already available; both were followed. Encouraged by the Earls of Bedford, Cornelius Vermuyden, a Dutch engineer, planned and directed the draining of 700,000 acres of fenland, bogs, pools, and reed shoals in the eastern counties, between 1626 and 1652, to produce what is still some of the richest farming land in England. During the next 150 years England was also fortunate in having a number of outstanding farmers, willing and able to experiment in the selection of better strains of grasses, in the introduction of new crops, in the rotation of crops, in the use of fertilizers, and in the methods of mixed farming, where crops and animals were closely interrelated.

To put many of these new methods into practice and produce the food for the now more rapidly growing population, another series of enclosures was necessary. By the beginning of the nineteenth century the land was almost entirely enclosed and the peasant system of farming had gone, to be replaced by larger units, on which the farmer, whether he was owner or tenant, employed hired labor.

With the nineteenth century came the industrial revolution. The population increased at an unprecedented rate, and the hordes of workers in the towns needed food and had money with which to buy it. Although many farmers responded by farming at a high level, and as a result enjoyed a period of great prosperity, they could not keep up with the demands for food from a population which grew roughly fourfold in a hundred years (from 8,892,536 in 1801 to 32,527,843 in 1901).

Once more, the only solutions were either to produce more on the land already farmed, or to bring more land into cultivation. At the time, there was little that could be done to increase the output from each available acre of land, nor was there land in Britain which, by draining or other treatment, could be brought economically into use.

Two other great changes were, however, taking place which made it possible to provide the essential food. New continents were being opened up, and steam power was making sea transport both more rapid and more certain. The North American continent and Australasia offered more than enough land to feed Britain's growing millions. If there had been no simultaneous advance in the ease and speed of sea transport, the only remedy to overpopulation would have been to export Britain's surplus millions along with their skills and the industries they served, until there remained at home only the number which could be supported by the produce of the land, together with any surpluses of food available from neighboring countries such as Ireland or Denmark.

In the new countries land was plentiful and often richly fertile, with the stored nutrients of centuries. Machines had been invented, particularly the binder, which made farming much less dependent on manual labor. These factors, together with cheap and quick sea transport, made possible a system which might be called "static nomadism." The methods used in opening up these new lands were essentially similar to those of the nomadic tribes. The settler cropped or stocked his land, without any rotation designed to maintain its fertility, until it was exhausted; when he could no longer grow a satisfactory crop he moved on to a new virgin area. He grew wheat year after year, or with an intervening fallow if the rainfall was inadequate, until the soil lost its fertility and became a heap of dust. The stock farmer grazed his herds and flocks on the native pasture. If he was content to have a light stocking and to maintain proper rotational grazing, the herbage regenerated quickly enough to provide a permanent farming system, but too often he was greedy and careless; because land was plentiful it was easier and more profitable to overgraze and exhaust a small area than to move his stock systematically over a large expanse of land.

It is interesting to speculate whether if Britain had exported all those who could not be fed from her own farms, this destruction of virgin land would not have taken place; stable balanced communities might have grown up, an industrial population side by side with the farms that fed it. But Britain sent only a relatively small number of settlers, primarily to farm and send back the food needed for her industrial workers at home. When the products of the land were being shipped to the other side of the world, it must have mattered little to many of these settlers if they exploited the land for immediate profit and moved to a new area whenever it became necessary. If the industries had been their neighbors, they would surely have seen the advantages of a permanent farming system; have adopted the rotations and mixed farming used in the land from which they came; and so have retained the fertility of their soil.

But the system of "static nomadism," in which the major part of the population remained at home in Britain while a relative few, together with settlers from other European countries, went overseas to produce food needed by those remaining at home, was immediately highly profitable, both to industrial Britain and to the countries of the American continents and Australasia. So profitable was it, indeed, that from 1880 onward more and more of Britain's food was imported, with a disastrous effect on her farming.

The later years of the reign of Victoria and those of Edward

VII saw industrial Britain at the peak of her prosperity. Men rich with the profits of industry invested in country estates, content to derive no financial return so long as they could enjoy the social prestige which sprang from the ownership of a country property; they were prepared to charge low rents to tenants who in turn were willing to consider the sporting and other amenities as of greater importance than the efficiency of their farming. The older landowners, who had no income apart from their investment in land, were forced to follow suit and lower their rents. Whereas, however, the wealthy industrialist maintained the buildings and amenities of his property, often in an unnecessarily lavish way, his fellow landlord with no outside source of income was forced to neglect the maintenance of his property and to allow it to fall into disrepair.

The farmer largely gave up the attempt to compete with cheap imported food. He cut his expenditure to a minimum; he pressed his landlord for even lower rents; he set aside the plow, the binder, and the threshing machine and allowed his land to revert to permanent pasture, much of it of poor quality; and he spent little or nothing on fertilizers and cut his labor force, paying his laborers the lowest wages of any craftsman.

Apart from a few specialized crops such as vegetables, fruit, and potatoes, the major product of British farming in the early years of the century was liquid milk, produced largely from stock given imported feed.

It has been necessary to stress the changes in farming in Britain up to the early years of the century, because they profoundly affected the development of farming throughout the world. Anyone surveying world agriculture immediately before World War I would have seen Britain using her industrial wealth to buy food from every part of the world: grain from the prairies of North America, from Australia, and from Southern Euope; meat again fom North America but also in steadily increasing quantities from New Zealand and the Argentine; butter from Denmark, Ireland, and New Zealand; and tropical products from Asia, Africa, and the West Indies. There was, of course, some exchange of foodstuffs among all the countries of the world, but Britain was the only major buyer with a population which had money to spend and which had outstripped its capacity or willingness to produce. As such it bought cheaply, particularly from those countries where the farmers were producing cheaply at the expense of their natural resources.

Although for the time being all may have appeared well, a closer inspection of the position would have indicated trouble for the future. The population of the United States was growing rapidly, and the foundations of her mammoth industries were already being laid. It seemed that the time must come when even her vast farmlands would no more than support her own people. What was happening in the United States must inevitably follow in the other great food-producing countries as their populations increased and turned to the manufacture of their own requirements and ultimately to the export of manufactured goods. If there had been no wars and no major developments in agricultural techniques, the time must have come in, say, fifty years, when there was no longer a surplus of cheap food for Britain to buy.

World War I gave Britain a sharp warning of the danger of her position, but it had only a transient effect so far as the politicians and farmers were concerned. Within a few years British agriculture was once more depressed and neglected and her people living on cheap imported food.

There was, however, another great force at work: the rapid development of science and engineering and the application of the products of research and invention in the improvement of farming techniques. The last half of the nineteenth century and the first decade of the twentieth had been marked by the rapid growth of the natural sciences and engineering. Many of these advances provided the basic knowledge on which a new and more productive agriculture could be built.

In the period between the wars, there was little to encourage the scientist to apply his skill to the problems of a depressed agriculture, but the age-old challenge was still there, to make two blades of grass grow where only one had grown before. Among scientists, too, there was greater appreciation of the threat of a world population which was fast outstripping the output from the land. The knowledge that many men, women, and children throughout the world were suffering from malnutrition and hunger, that there was not enough food in the world, and that apparent surpluses were only the result of maldistribution was probably the greatest spur to the scientists engaged in research on the problems concerned with increased food production. Whatever the stimulus, the results achieved since the beginning of the century have been dramatic; there has been a revolution in agriculture, and the potential output from each acre of land and from each man has been greatly increased.

One of the major factors in crop production is the supply of plant nutrients. Provided an adequate supply of water is available, as well as the necessary warmth and light, the yield from a plant is limited by the mineral nutrients available. Chemists had established by the early years of the nineteenth century that the three main elements required were phosphorus, potassium, and nitrogen. All these could be supplied from animal excreta and rotting vegetation. When all the animal and human excreta and waste vegetation were returned to the land, as they were in primitive village communities, there was a more or less closed cycle from which there was little loss; any such loss was made good by the breakdown of minerals in the soil to provide phosphates and potassium salts and by the fixation of nitrogen from the air by bacteria. There resulted a steady, but low, level of crop yields. When, however, crops and animal products were taken from the village and used to feed the population of cities, there was a continuous loss of nutrients. If this were greater than the natural replacement, there was an inevitable slow fall in fertility and hence in yield.

Means had to be found to make good these losses. Phosphates and potassium could be supplied by the use of minerals rich in these elements, either in their natural state or treated to render them more easily available to the plant. Nitrogen could be supplied by encouraging in the crop rotation legumes, whose root nodules fixed atmospheric nitrogen. By these means crop yields were maintained throughout the nineteenth century. In Britain, for example, the yields of cereals showed little or no change between 1880 and 1930, although the use of mineral fertilizers had been rising slowly.

As towns and cities grew and modern sewage systems were introduced, loss of plant nutrients increased. Another factor adversely affecting the nutritional status of the soil was the replacement of horse transport by the automobile. It had been the custom for carts bringing farm produce to the London markets to return loaded with horse manure from the city stables. At the same time the farm horse was giving way to the tractor. Phosphates and potassium were available in plenty in mineral deposits to replace these losses, but there was no such natural source of nitrogen. In the temperate, heavily populated European countries where the yield from the land had to be maintained year after year, an alternative source of nitrogen was essential.

Advances in physical chemistry and in chemical engineering supplied the answer in the processes for fixing the nitrogen of the air in readily usable forms. Now there was the means not only of maintaining yields but, where the water supply and other physical conditions were right, of materially increasing them. But throughout the Great Depression of the 1930's there seemed no point in pushing up yields: money was not available to buy more food at economic prices.

The release of agriculture from the straitjacket of a limited nitrogen supply posed new problems. Many of the crop varieties which had served farmers well in the past did not meet the new conditions of heavy fertilizer application. New varieties were needed that would be capable of responding to these conditions and have an anatomic structure suited to carrying the heavier crop.

Advances in the science of genetics put in the hands of the plant breeders the means of creating new varieties, designed to suit the new conditions. Once the plant breeders had realized their new powers, however, they embarked on new adventures of their own, and by using factors such as hybrid vigor produced new plant varieties with greater yields than the old when the two were grown under identical conditions.

A higher level of farming called for the protection of the crop from pests and diseases and from the competition of weeds for water and plant nutrients. A farmer who spent money on fertilizers and on good seed could not afford to have his crop eaten by pests or ruined by disease, nor could he permit it to be smothered with weeds.

The chemical industry took up the challenge of crop protection and produced a wide range of insecticides and fungicides which have given the farmer the means of controlling many of the worst enemies of his crops.

The automobile has brought about another change, this time in social conditions. When the horse was the only means of transport in many rural areas, men lived out their lives in a village, with an occasional visit to a neighboring country town where they met only their fellow farm workers. With the advent of the automobile, townsmen found their way into the country and countrymen into the towns. The farm workers and their wives learned of higher wages and shorter hours in industry and of the amenities of town life. The farmer could not meet a higher wage bill in the period of depression, so his workers drifted off hopefully to the towns — often to join the unemployed there — and the farmer managed with fewer men. The engineer had made this possible by providing a wide range of machines which could replace hand labor. These in turn created their own economic problems in countries where farms were small and the individual ownership of an expensive machine could not be justified.

From this has grown a movement for the amalgamation of holdings into larger units which in turn makes the more rapid application of new knowledge possible. The historian of the future may see this as the elimination of the small farmer, just as the advances at the time of the eighteenth-century enclosures eliminated the peasant.

There was one activity on the farm in which the machine could not fully replace manual labor, namely, the control of weeds. Here again the scientist came to the farmer's aid. In the years between the wars, chemists had been experimenting with various chemicals as weed killers, but not until World War II did plant physiologists and biochemists evolve the principle on which the modern range of selective herbicides is based. The power to control weeds in his growing crops completed for the time being the farmer's requirements for producing high yields.

When the World War II disrupted the transport of Britain's food supplies for the second time, there were both the need and the opportunity to put these new techniques into practice, but it was not until the postwar period that dramatic increases in production took place. Between 1946 and 1956, average cereal yields rose by 25 per cent and potatoes by roughly 15 per cent. The average yield of wheat in Britain is now around 25 cwt. (46 bushels) to the acre; the best farmers on good land expect to get an average of not less than 2 tons (75 bushels) and many are looking forward confidently to yields of over 100 bushels.

The better management of pastures, grown as part of a rotation with proper fertilizers and weed control, has resulted at the same time in similar increases in animal products from grass.

Pigs and poultry are being bred more scientifically and managed and fed with greater knowledge and skill. Veterinary medicine has eliminated many of the most serious losses from disease. The over-all result of these scientific developments in agriculture has been to lift the net output of British farms to 160 per cent of the prewar figure, on a diminishing acreage and with a fall of more than 15 per cent in the labor force.

Britain is not unique in the application of these new farming techniques; it is, however, unique in that the farmers have been actively stimulated by the government to these higher levels of production. In many of the more highly developed countries the techniques have been freely adopted by the farmers, often with resulting embarrassing surpluses. In the less developed countries (which are discussed later), the standard of production has remained deplorably low, and it is here that population increases make more efficient food production vital to the well-being of the people.

World agriculture today presents a strange picture. The world population it has to feed is increasing at an alarming rate, and more than half its present numbers are undernourished. In the countries of high productivity and relatively low population density, there are embarrassing surpluses. In those with low productivity and high population densities, there is acute shortage, and by and large these countries do not have the funds to buy what is in excess elsewhere. They can get part of what they need only as generous gifts of surpluses. Clearly, the first task is to try to raise the standard of farming in these hungry countries, by applying the techniques which have already been proven elsewhere. But, while this might meet the needs of the world population today, in the years it will take to achieve such an end the number of mouths to be fed will have jumped still further ahead. Until the growth in population can be checked, agriculture will always be chasing a receding objective.

Scientific research directed to the improvement of agriculture is concentrated in countries with a high level of productivity and with actual or potential surpluses. It is to be expected, therefore, that the main efforts will be toward reducing the cost of production, utilizing surpluses, and finding marketable crops which can be grown as an alternative.

The pressure to solve these problems of immediate economic importance should not be allowed to blind us to the need for research directed to finding means for increasing the output from every acre of land capable of producing food.

It will be necessary to bring to bear on the problem all the knowledge and every technique available to the scientist. The last great leap forward in productivity, based on the scientific advances of the first half of the twentieth century, has now reached a plateau beyond which the best farmers can go little further.

Before agriculture can become more productive, it must await the application of the findings of a new field of science which will open up entirely new approaches to the old problems which have so far proved insoluble. Nuclear physics and its many applications in chemistry and biology provides just such an opening. This has been grasped by research workers with great enthusiasm, and radioactive elements have found a place in every branch of agricultural research. It is too early yet to do more than speculate on the ultimate effect on food production of investigations in which radioactive substances are employed, but some examples will illustrate the great potential influence of this work.

One of the unsolved problems of fertilizer practice is the behavior of phosphates in the soil. When phosphatic fertilizers are added to soil, they react with other soil constituents and in part are rendered unavailable to the plant. Each year the farmer adds fresh fertilizer so that it is available for his crop, and each year part of this disappears into the soil complex; but it is not entirely lost to the plant. When a sufficient reserve of unavailable phosphate has been built up, the process can be reversed, if the level of available phosphate falls. Thus, Dutch farmers found during the war, when no phosphatic fertilizers were available, that they had a sufficient reserve in the soil from past applications to meet the requirements of their crops without any drop in yield. It is obviously of great importance to the farmer to know more about the behavior of phosphates in soil, if this means that he can omit their use in some years.

The study of this problem has been limited in the past by the scientist's inability to follow the fate of added phosphorus. The us of the radioactive isotope $P^{32}$ has opened up new lines of investigation. Not only is it possible to follow experimentally the fate of added phosphate in contact with different soils but also, by feeding radioactive phosphate to soil and following its absorption by the plant, the relative proportions of the total phosphate uptake coming from the added material and from the fixed phosphate in the soil can be determined.

Another problem of great importance to the farmer is the crop density which gives him the maximum yield. If the spacings are too close, the plants interfere with each other and growth is hindered; if they are too far apart, land and fertilizer are wasted. Scientists have been studying root development for many years, but with limited success. Any experiments involved either digging up the plants in order to examine the roots or artificial conditions such as boxes with glass sides through which a section of the roots of the plant could be seen.

A simple solution to this problem is again provided by the use of $P^{32}$. A solution of phosphate containing $P^{32}$ is placed in the soil at different distances from the plant and at different depths below it. As soon as a root meets this radioactive materials, it can be detected in the growing tips of the plant. By placing the radioactive material in different positions for successive plants, it is possible to form a good picture of the root development.

There are many other ways in which radioactive tracers can be used to elucidate the complex mechanisms of photosynthesis and plant nutrition, all of which are adding to the general store of fundamental knowledge on which those engaged in applied research will draw in the future.

The solution of many problems complementary to those of plant nutrition, namely, those concerned with plant protection, can be found in the use of radioactive tracers.

It is often difficult to follow the movements of small winged insects and to study their feeding habits. Where these insects are the vectors carrying disease it is of the greatest importance to know how far and in what way they travel. If they are allowed to feed on a plant which has been labeled with $P^{32}$ it is comparatively easy to follow the pattern and distance of their movements and then to design more effective means for their control. The movements of burrowing insects and nematodes are equally difficult to follow without the use of radioactive tracers, but a few microcuries of a gamma-emitting isotope attached to the body of a wire worm will enable its movements to be traced easily and plans can then be laid for its destruction.

Radioactive tracers are also used to study the efficiency of spraying, the movement of systemic insecticides within the plant, and the persistence of poisonous insecticides and fungicides on edible crops. In fact, there are infinite ways in which tracers can be used in the study of crop production and protection.

A more direct use of radiation in insect control has been developed by the United States Department of Agriculture. Suitable exposure of male insects to a cobalt-60 source renders them sterile. If, as with many insects, the female mates only once, the release of large numbers of sterile males will result in a corresponding number of females laying infertile eggs. This technique requires massive organization and must be carried out where there can be no heavy reinfection of the treated area. It has been used successfully against screw worm — a serious pest of cattle —in Curaçao and more recently in Florida.

Radioactive sources, too, have their place in plant breeding, although here the early promise has not been entirely fulfilled. When seeds or growing buds are exposed to nuclear radiations, mutations occur. Many of these mutants have been so changed that they will not survive, but among those that do there may be found desirable characteristics which can be introduced by breeding into commercial varieties. Mass irradiation was tried by the use of a powerful cobalt-60 source in a field where the various crops could be grown at suitable distances. However, this method requires elaborate equipment and organization and is apt to produce, when the seeds are grown on, an embarrassing number of mutations, which present enormous problems to the plant breeder. It is very rare that a mutant retains the good qualities of the parent strain with an added desirable character. Almost always the desirable character is associated with undesirable variations, and hence a long breeding program is involved in fixing the new character in a new variety which also has all the good qualities of the old. Most plant breeders are content to use irradiation at relatively low levels and on a small scale. Seeds or pollen grains are exposed to a modest source of a few curies in a rotating container. Such a technique yields no more mutants than can be easily handled.

In the study of animal metabolism there is also a wide range of uses for radioactive isotopes. The path for the synthesis of milk fats has been elucidated by the use of isotopically labeled short-chain fatty acids. Radioactive magnesium has been used in the study of hypomagnesemia, a serious metabolic disease of cattle. Calcium-45 and strontium-89 have been used to study the metabolism of these elements in mountain sheep on different dietary levels. Cobalt-58 is used in the study of the role of vitamin $B_{12}$ in metabolism. The labeling of protein by iodine-131 has enabled important studies to be made of the transfer of antibodies from mother to offspring in different animals.

These are all indirect contributions to the increase of agricultural productivity. With the urgent need for more food, we must ask ourselves if there are no immediate and large-scale applications of nuclear physics which can serve to increase our food supplies. The answer is, unfortunately, "No." It may be that in the distant future cheap nuclear power will enable us to tame deserts and to grow food in the far north, but for many years to come, radioactive substances will be tools in the hands of the scientists who, by a multiplicity of independent discoveries, will enable the farmer to grow heavier crops and to get greater yields from his livestock.

To sum up, agriculture has so far succeeded in meeting at least in part the demands for food of the world's population. It could do still more if farming could be raised to a uniformly high level, but that depends on political, economic, and sociological changes. Beyond that, it must await new scientific knowledge which will enable the best farmers, who are already making use of every gift from science, to increase still further their already high yields.

CHAPTER

**3**

# FOOD AND FOOD PROCESSING

**M**AN MUST HAVE an adequate and well-balanced diet if he
is to lead an active and healthy life, but to achieve a full
life he must also find pleasure in his food. The old saying that
we should eat to live, not live to eat, represents a puritanical
attitude engendered by the gluttony of our wealthier forefathers.
The French have always taken a more sophisticated attitude
toward food, thinking more of its excellence than of its quantity
and being quite unashamedly concerned with the pleasures of
the table.

With the development of the science of nutrition, we cannot
but be aware of the importance of the different constituents of
a balanced diet. We are conscious of the need for high-quality
protein, vitamins, and minerals, and many of us spend unnecessary time and energy, to say nothing of money, in making sure
that they are all included in our food. A good plain diet of the
type eaten in the Western world should contain them all. Where
it does not, the fault often lies in the overrefinement of some
item or in bad methods of processing. Having taken an essential
factor out of our diet, we proceed to put it back, not infrequently
at considerable cost.

Modern knowledge about the dangers of pathogenic micro-organisms has produced in many an acute fear of any food which appears to have suffered bacteriological or enzymic change, yet many foods are hardly edible until such changes have taken place.

It must be our aim to take the food from the farm or the sea and present it on the table with as small a loss in nutritional value as possible and in a condition which gives the greatest gastronomic pleasure, in order to stimulate the appetite. To do so involves storing and processing a large part of our food.

In our modern world, where the great masses of the people live in large towns, few foods are eaten in their natural state. Even where it is not processed, food must be stored or transported long distances if there is to be a continuous supply throughout the year. Whether such a supply is obtained by storing the locally produced foods until they are needed, or by bringing food as it is required from parts of the world where it is currently being harvested, some degree of preservation is involved.

Only for a very short time in the year can we eat a few foods fresh from the field or garden, raw, and untreated in any way. When a larger part of the population lived on the land, our ancestors ate perhaps a little more fresh unprocessed food, but by no means as much as we are apt to assume. With few exceptions, they had to live on the produce of their own land and hence to store food in summer for winter use. Many of the products of the farm could not be stored without some form of processing; pickling, preserving, drying, and salting were the accepted duties of the country housewife, as were brewing, baking, and making butter and cheese.

Yet for all his efforts to preserve food and his nearness to the land, the peasant, before imported foods and modern methods of preservation became available, was living on an ill-balanced diet.

Only for a short time in summer, when fresh fruits were available, could he have had an adequate supply of vitamin C. The few vegetables he ate during the rest of the year did not contain any adequate amounts of the vitamin, and the rest of his diet of salt meat, bread, and dried peas contributed little or nothing.

In medieval towns the position was worse. Here there was less fresh fruit available, so that even in the summer the diet remained deficient in vitamin C. The greater part of the population in town and country alike must have been in a scorbutic or pre-scorbutic — sub-scurvy — condition. The correction of this fault in our diet has slowly come about as transport has made more fresh fruits and vegetables available and better methods of processing have retained the vitamin content in preserved foodstuffs. Even among the wealthier part of the population, pre-scorbutic conditions were prevalent in the seventeenth century. Evelyn, gives an interesting example of this in his diary, in the entry for May 7, 1662. He describes how a man subjected his arm to Mr. Boyle's vacuum and how on "drawing it out, we found it all speckled." The weakening of the walls of the capillary blood vessels which caused this speckling is a well-recognized symptom of the pre-scorbutic condition.

The lack of green vegetables for man and of green fodder for dairy cattle led to a deficiency of vitamin A in the diet. It may have been partly offset by the consumption of the animal viscera, particularly the liver and kidneys. The supplies of this vitamin were probably more nearly sufficient in the diet of the rich towns-man, who ate large quantities of animal fats. There is no doubt, however, that such symptoms of vitamin-A deficiency as night blindness were prevalent. It is also possible that lack of vitamin A together with a high intake of calcium was responsible for the wide incidence of stones in the bladder and urinary tract.

Parallel to the deficiency of vitamin A there was most probably a lack of vitamin D. Much depended, however, on the inclusion of milk and milk products in the diet. If these were high, as they were in some country districts, the intake may have been adequate. In the towns, however, and among the wealthier classes

who despised the so-called white meats there must have been
a shortage of this vitamin. Although it was not until the industrial revolution in England, when people were crowded into the
towns with inadequate supplies of milk, milk products, and meat,
that serious vitamin-D deficiency in the form of rickets became
common, there is evidence that it was prevalent in Europe in
medieval times. Many paintings of the Virgin and Child show
in the infant the typical pot belly and crooked legs of rickets.
Although this cannot be regarded as definite evidence of the general incidence of the condition — there was too much copying
of conventional forms for the repetition of the type to be entirely
significant — it gives support to the limited, but more scientific
and detailed, evidence of the early medical writers.

It is important to look back on the conditions existing before
food storage and preservation were known as they are today. So
often it is said that we suffer from eating food of which the nutritive value and taste have been destroyed or reduced on the passage from the farm to the table, that we forget the alternative
would often be the complete loss of these foods and the return of
the resulting deficiency diseases, which we have long ceased to
fear.

Apart from the absence of many important foods from the
tables of our forefathers, we should, if we were set down to dine
with them, be disgusted at the condition of much we had to eat.
Many components of the meal we should frankly regard as rotten
and inedible; the bread full of weevils and other insects and
sour with mold, the milk sour, the butter rancid, the apples with-
ered with storage, and the meat so freshly killed as to be tough
and tasteless.

Among the many micro-organisms attacking the food would
be some which were pathogenic. Those of our forefathers who
survived in early life were probably largely immune, but a terrible
toll was taken of babies and young children. The conditions existing among the poorer classes in the Western world virtually up

to the end of the nineteenth century differed only in severity from those we find today in many parts of the East. The ravages of infantile diarrhea and other intestinal disorders, together with malnutrition and tuberculosis, are only too well recorded on the tombstones in many an English churchyard.

Nonetheless, these were the ills to which the people were accustomed; they were acts of God, to be suffered in patience. When, however, the scientists began to correct them by applying their new-won knowledge to the storage and preservation of food, every error was magnified and resented. These were not the acts of God, but the failings of man, an attitude of which still persists today.

There is a feeling abroad that so long as naturally occurring substances are used in storage and processing, and the only treatment is heating for drying or cooking, no great harm can be done to the nutritive value of food; but that any use of "chemicals" or processes such as canning, evaporation, or irradiation must, because they are new, be risky and probably positively harmful. Much of this opposition arises from early mistakes made in new methods of processing, and to the fact that our palates have become accustomed to the flavors arising from treatments with impure substances — in the chemical sense — and from the products of bacterial action in partially decayed foodstuffs.

The history of canning serves to illustrate the thorny path of the innovator in food processing. Canning had its origin long before Pasteur had revealed the part played by micro-organisms, not only in fermentation but also in putrefaction. At the beginning of the nineteenth century it was thought that if food could be sealed in an air-free container, it would keep in a fresh condition, air being considered the cause of putrefaction. Two workers, Appert in France and Saddington in England, succeeded in preserving a wide range of foods in glass bottles by heating them in a hot-water bath. Although Appert's bottles were sealed before heating, he still thought it was the exclusion of air which pre-vented putrefaction. Saddington's method was almost identical with that used in the domestic bottling of fruit today. The stop-pers of his bottles were loose-fitting; after heating to 160°-170° F. the bottles were filled with hot water and tightly closed. Both methods were successful on a small scale.

The next step was to use tinned iron canisters, leaving a small hole which could be sealed after heating with a dab of solder. Donkin in England perfected this process by 1812 and was soon supplying the Navy and Arctic explorers with meat and vege-tables preserved in canisters of 2 to 6 lb. in weight. The business was so successful that others joined in, with the almost inevitable result that mistakes were made and the process was discredited. The first trouble arose from lack of scientific knowledge of what was happening in the containers. A manufacturer, Stephen Gold-ner, who had been canning meat satisfactorily in small containers, increased the size to between 9 and 14 lb. Reports began to come in of meats not keeping properly. The complaints grew; in 1850 over 100,000 lb. of Goldner's meat was condemned in one Ad-miralty yard alone, and he lost his contract. If Goldner had known that his process depended on meat sterilization, the solu-tion to the problem would have been obvious. In the absence of this knowledge it took some years and a Select Committee to discover that it was the large tins which were causing the trouble. Even then the reason, that in the large tins the meat was not ster-ilized in the center, was not known. It was not until ten years later that Calvert in his Cantor Lectures at the Society of Arts pointed out the significance of Pasteur's work in relation to meat canning.

When the scare caused by Goldner's failure had died down, another difficulty arose in the path of the canning industry. Aus-tralian packers began to send meat to England. The tins of meat were cheap and there was no decomposition, but the quality of the meat itself was very poor. It was described as consisting of a lump of coarse, tough, lean meat with a large lump of coarse fat and a thin watery fluid. Even to the poor, hungry workers of those times the contents were repulsive. Unfortunately, canned meats of all kinds suffered from the revulsion of the public to this poor-quality material. The general reaction to canned meat in the 1860's is well illustrated by the morbid joke of the sailors at Portsmouth, who dubbed the product of the victualing yard at Dartmouth "Sweet Fanny Adams." The lady in question was a victim of a sensational murder of the time, her body having been hacked to small pieces by her murderer. Those who served in World War I will remember that the expression was then still used by the troops.

The reputation of canned meats was further harmed by the reaction between minute traces of sulphur compounds given off by some meats and the metal surface of the container. This produced a darkening of the contents or, in extreme cases, black stains. This discoloration, although harmless, gave the impression of decomposition, and it was not until the beginning of this century that the cause was discovered and remedied by lacquering the inside of the tins.

When the anti-scorbutic vitamins were discovered, it was found that the canning process then in use led to their loss. The public, still with memories of the previous troubles, was only too ready to believe that canned fruits and vegetables had lost much of their nutritive qualities. The American canning industry, which by this time was pre-eminent in the world, spent large sums of money on research and showed that the loss was due to oxidation, and that if the cans were filled as full as possible and the remaining air driven out quickly, there was no loss of vitamin A.

Fear of decomposition in the tin has created in the public mind the suspicion that canned meats are one of the major causes of food poisoning. This is quite unfounded. Cases of food poisoning have been caused by canned food, particularly meat, but most of these have resulted from home canning, where the amateur was unable to control the temperature effectively and the contents were not fully sterilized.

The modern commercial product is prepared from high-quality raw materials, partly because the canner provides one of the farmer's best markets and partly because it is uneconomical to spend money on canning inferior material. The process is strictly controlled at each stage, and the final product is not released for sale until it has passed severe tests. It is fair to say that canned food today is fully as nutritive as many of the fresh products sold to the public, and has a better record for purity and freedom from food poisoning. Modern methods of transport and distribution have greatly improved the quality of fresh food on sale, but where older, less efficient, and less hygienic systems still prevail, the canned product is better in quality and freer from possible bacterial contamination, and retains a much higher proportion of the original nutritive value of the raw material than the product which is allegedly fresh.

The next advance in canning may well be the use of gamma rays to sterilize cooked meats in sealed containers. A large source is required to provide the 100,000 roentgens (r) which are needed to destroy the micro-organisms present and to inactivate the enzymes.

There are three difficulties to be surmounted before this method can be put into general use. Sources capable of providing the levels of radiation required are difficult to handle and present a danger to the workers. The cobalt-60 used for experimental work of this type at the Atomic Energy Research Establishment at Wantage in Britain is housed in a temperature-controlled room which is entered through a labyrinth to prevent the escape of scattered gamma rays. The cobalt-60, when it is not in use, is housed in a thicker portion of the concrete wall. It can be lowered into the reaction room only when the operator has left and closed and locked the entry gate, after making sure that no one is left in the room. Such an arrangement is obviously very expensive. A simpler arrangement can be made in which the tins travel on a conveyer belt past the source, but such a system, although simpler in principle, is costly to install. That at the Wantage Laboratory will deliver 2,000,000 r to about two and one-half tons of meat per day, a small total for so large and complicated a piece of equipment.

The second difficulty is economic, arising from the present high cost of the equipment. Unless there were a material commercial advantage, e.g., better keeping qualities in the irradiated product, the cost could not be justified.

Although there is already evidence that meat treated by this process will keep longer than meat canned by the ordinary processes, there are other factors which tend to make it less acceptable. The irradiation process produces different flavors and smells as the result of the breakdown of organic substances in the meat. Many of these are objectionable and could well be associated in the public mind with bacterial decomposition products. It is absolutely essential that this difficulty should be overcome before any irradiated canned meat is put on the market. Work directed to eliminating these off-flavors and smells is going on in many laboratories, and progress has already been made. The use of anti-oxidants is one techique; another is the use of charcoal as an absorbent. The addition of anti-oxidants has the disadvantage that it may revive the erroneous idea that the addition of preservatives forms a part of the canning process. Moreover, the addition of any new chemical substance to food immediately raises the question of whether it is safe. It may be established that while it is not poisonous in the narrow sense of the word, there still remains the possibility of cumulative and long-term effects. The method of absorption on charcoal would appear to be more promising, but until the cost can be brought down at least to the level of the present commercial process, there seems little possibility of irradiation being adopted on the grounds that a superior product results.

Milk is one of our most valuable foods. The nutrients it contains have been preserved from the earliest times, in the forms of butter, cheese, and whey. Milk, together with these products, formed a major part of the "white meats" so important in the medieval peasant's diet. Yet milk has been one of the main carriers of disease, particularly to town populations. Until the middle of the nineteenth century the milk supply to the large industrial towns in Britain, particularly London, was unbelievably bad. Cows were kept in town dairies, without light or ventilation, knee-deep in filth, and with an entirely inadequate diet. The milk was contaminated with blood and pus, and its bacterial content must have been astronomically high.

From 1850, London increasingly drew its milk supply from the country; the newly built railways bringing it in from the eastern counties. Faced by this competition, and suffering from the great outbreak of rinderpest between 1863 and 1867, many of the town dairies were put out of business. From then on they gradually dwindled in number, although a few survived until the beginning of this century.

The milk coming in from the country was often heavily contaminated with bacteria, and long journeys by train, particularly in the summer, meant that much was already partially soured when it was delivered to the customer. Also, the dairymen watered much of the milk. The only test then in use was by the lactometer to determine the specific gravity and by adding water and removing fat, they could keep the specific gravity within the legal range. When chemical methods for determining the fat content were brought into use, the fraud could be detected. The average value for the fat content of London milk in 1865 was found by Voelker to be 2.17 per cent, with some samples as low as 1.75 per cent, compared with a normal average value of 3.65 per cent. The poor quality of milk coming from the country as delivered by the dairymen helped to develop a fashion in the later years of the nineteenth century for drinking milk warm from the cow in some London dairies.

By 1890 the work of Pasteur had led to the introduction of the process known by his name. This was first introduced not to control pathogenic organisms but to prevent souring, by killing the acid-forming bacteria. However, in less than ten years the value of pasteurization was recognized as protection against milk-borne diseases. The process as first applied was very crude; some of the milk would be overheated and given a "cooked" flavor, while another batch would be underheated and so remain a danger to health.

Although pasteurization plants were improved in the early twentieth century, it was not until after World War I that the installations became generally reliable. As a result, there was strong opposition to pasteurization in Britain for a long time. In spite of the known danger from bovine tuberculosis and other milk-borne diseases, the compulsory pasteurization of milk was strongly resisted, on the grounds that the nutritive value was impaired and the flavor was unpleasant. It was once again the same story as in canning; the early imperfections of the process had created prejudices which were difficult to overcome. Scientific evidence of the nutritive value of pasteurized milk carried little weight against firmly rooted conviction. The production of "certified" and "tuberculin-tested" milk was encouraged, with elaborate cowshed hygiene and the regular tuberculin testing of the dairy herd, but until the 1950's, raw milk from untested herds was still widely sold.

About ten years ago, following the example set in some states of the United States, the sale of raw milk was limited by law in Britain to attested herds, that is, herds maintained free from tuberculosis; all other milk had to be either pasteurized or sterilized. The latter category was introduced to meet the demand in some areas for milk with longer keeping qualities.

At the same time a scheme was initiated for the eradication of tubercular cattle. This has now been completed, so that the fear of contamination from bovine tuberculosis has been eliminated. The need for protection against other diseases carried in milk is now well recognized, and by far the larger part of the milk in Britain is handled by the large dairies and pasteurized; the rest has to conform to rigid bacteriological standards.

Attempts have been made to use irradiation as a means of sterilizing milk, but so far these have not proved competitive with modern commercial methods of pasteurization.

The failures of early efforts to keep and transport meat, fruit, and vegetables by heat sterilization turned attention to the possibility of preserving perishable foods without sterilization, by reducing the bacterial and enzymic activity through storage at a low temperature. There was nothing new in this idea. It had been practiced from the earliest times, but it could not be attempted on a large scale until a suitable regular supply of ice was available. The use of ammonia gas as a refrigerant by the French engineer Carré provided the means for obtaining such a supply, and an ice plant was set up in Sydney in 1861 to produce 8,000 lb. of ice a day. There still were many problems to solve before the transport of meat in large quantities could become a commercial success. Harrison, working in Melbourne, succeeded in keeping whole carcasses of beef and mutton in an icehouse, cooled by a mixture of ice and salt, for several months. When, however, he tried to repeat this success in 1873, in the hold of a ship on a three-month voyage to England, the result was a complete disaster. The ice melted in the tropics and most of the meat had to be jettisoned during the voyage; what remained when the ship docked in England was no longer fit to eat. It soon became evident that the freezing equipment must be installed in the ship and that the cooling must be not by direct contact with ice but by brine circulated in pipes around the chamber in which the meat was packed. A number of partially successful shipments were made from the Argentine to France, but it was not until 1880 that a cargo of meat from Australia arrived in sufficiently good condition to be sold in Smithfield market in London.

The early cargoes of frozen meat, although they were fit to eat, were far from appetizing. There was marked "drip" of clear fluid and the meat tended to be flabby and dark in color. The flavor, too, was variable.

Slowly, the biochemistry and biophysics of the processes involved in meat storage were discovered and the quality of the product improved. The enzymes occurring in the living tissues are still present in the meat. The fat-splitting enzymes produce rancidity, the oxidative enzymes bleaching and a tallow-like character. The proteolytic enzymes produce a softening of the protein and so have a beneficial effect in rendering the meat more tender; it is in order to allow this action to take place that meat should be hung for some time before it is eaten.The aim must be to allow these enzyme reactions to proceed far enough for the meat to become tender but not far enough for the effects of other enzymes to become noticeable.

However carefully the meat is handled there must be some microbial infection which, if unchecked, will lead to mold formation, slime, and an offensive smell. Meat also loses water during storage, unless the humidity is kept high. This spoils the appearance of the meat but at the same time helps to prevent damage by bacteria and molds.

In a cold store there are three variable factors, temperature, humidity, and the composition of the atmosphere, which can be used to control these physical and chemical changes in the meat.

The temperature, and the rate at which it is reached, is all-important. If the meat is frozen down to $14°$ F., the growth of micro-organisms is inhibited and the enzymic reactions so reduced that the resulting changes are not noticeable over long periods. If, however, the meat is frozen slowly down to this temperature, irreversible changes due to the formation of large crystals of ice take place in the structure, and when thawed the meat becomes flabby and "drips" a watery fluid. If much higher temperatures are used, as in chilling, the meat in this system being kept at 29.5° F., the period during which it will remain fresh is not more than thirty days. This period can, however, be increased to fifty days if the concentration of carbon dioxide in the atmosphere is kept at between 10 and 12 per cent. The carbon dioxide prevents the microbial deterioration which is primarily responsible for the relatively short period over which meat can be kept at temperatures just below freezing point. Beef chilled in this way is shipped to Britain in large quantities from the southern hemisphere and is indistinguishable in condition from home-killed meat. It is, however, a relatively expensive process, the carcasses being hung and wrapped during transport. It is obviously foolish to use this system for anything but good-quality meat. Not only does the product in the butcher's shop reflect directly the quality of the original carcass, but in addition better-quality, well-finished, fine-grained, and well-handled meat appears to survive the chilling process better than the poorer material.

Bad fish has a peculiarly repulsive character of its own. Moreover, it reaches this obnoxious condition more rapidly than most other foods. Caught fish must in addition travel from the fishing grounds to the market. With in-shore fishing this may represent only one journey, from the fishing port to the town market, but when fish are caught on distant banks by trawlers, it may be up to two weeks before they reach market. It has, therefore, been the custom either to process fish by drying and smoking it or to pack it with ice for the fresh fish market. The block of ice on the fish-monger's slab and the broken ice in fish boxes were common sights in Britain long before the butchers thought of installing refrigerators.

It was also in connection with the preservation of fish that the importance of the rate of freezing was first observed and the explanation given that the better quality of rapidly frozen fish was due to the smaller size of the ice crystals formed. A number of workers in the years between the wars determined the optimum rates of cooling, and equipment was developed capable of achieving these rates.

The position, however, remained confused because other factors were involved besides the rate at which the temperature was lowered. The first of these was the treatment of the fish before freezing. Much of it had been stored in ice for days before the temperature was taken down to the final level. It has been shown that white-fleshed fish should not be stored in ice for longer than two days, if it is to be satisfactorily frozen. With herring the time is even shorter; they are not normally gutted after catching and sometimes can show marked deterioration within a few hours because of the bacteria and enzymes in the gut. As a general rule, herring must be frozen within twenty-four hours of catching.

The fishing industry of the future will have to range ever more widely for its catch, as more fish is required for the world's growing population. This can only mean an increasing interval between the time the fish is caught and when it is landed. If it is kept in ice during this period, it will not be suitable for freezing, nor can it be said that fish kept for a week or more in ice is more than edible; it has lost all the delightful flavor of freshly caught fish.

The ideal method of handling fish would undoubtedly be to gut and freeze the fish at sea. If fish could be frozen quickly, immediately after catching, that is, in not more than two hours, to a uniform temperature throughout of 23° F. and then stored at temperatures near 0° F., it would retain its initial freshness for several months. The length of storage life would vary with the type of fish and the final storage temperature, but at 0° F.

gutted white-fleshed fish would keep for a period of some four months.

The future fishing fleet may well consist, like a whaling fleet, of a number of trawlers feeding a factory ship where the catch would be immediately gutted, frozen, and packed down tight in the hold. The waste material could be dried down to fish meal and stored. At the present time trawlers from Britain have to steam hard to get their catch into port in reasonable condition; this affects their design and running costs. It also limits the time the trawlers can stay at sea. If the fishing is bad, the trawler may have to return with half a catch in order to land what has been caught before it goes bad. With a fleet of trawlers working to a large factory ship, the trawlers could be built to steam only slowly and to stay at sea for much longer periods. The factory ship itself need not be fast. It might be possible to have two such ships shuttling between the fishing fleet and the home port, bringing out relief crews and fuel and other supplies for the trawlers and taking back the men who had been relieved with their catch. It has been calculated that such a system would result in considerable reduction in running costs and would enable fish to reach the most distant inland towns in perfect condition. It would also, because the fish could be kept for a period of months, help to even out the gluts and shortages which now occur and would give the fisherman a steady price for his fish and the housewife a product of uniformly high quality. All that prevents the quick adoption of this system is the large capital investment in the present trawler fleet and the conservatism of the industry. The trawler skipper is a rugged individualist, proud of his skill, who thrives on competition and regards cooperation with suspicion. Such a system might also open up the possibility of sterilization at sea by the use of a radioactive source. Work is already in progress on this method of preservation, but much more will be needed before it is ready for commercial application.

The use of low temperatures for the preservation of food

stands less chance of running into ill-informed prejudice than most other forms of food storage and preservation. Nothing is added, the broad principle is known and practiced by everyone, and when the process is successful the end product is almost indistinguishable from the fresh material. Storage at low temperatures is, however, by no means simple and straightforward. Meat, fish, fruit, vegetables, and more recently cooked food, often in the form of already prepared meals, are being marketed in increasing quantities all over the world. Just as the preservation of meat and fish has been achieved only after prolonged experiment, so the storage of every other product has called for research and pilot scale experiment. A technique suited to one product may be quite useless for another.

Storage of apples and other similar hard fruits cannot be achieved by freezing. There are few apples which do not suffer from low-temperature injury at temperatures below 38° F. The storage life at this temperature is quite short. Those who try to store the apples from their garden in a cold cellar know that by January half of those remaining develop rots and have to be thrown away, a loss that could not be accepted in commercial storage. The food scientist therefore had to find some means of avoiding large-scale losses at the higher temperatures and injury which renders the fruit unmarketable at the lower. The solution to the dilemma was found in gas storage. If the content of carbon dioxide in the store is allowed to rise and that of oxygen to fall, the storage life of the apples is greatly increased and temperatures of 38°-40° F. can be used. Unfortunately, almost every commercial variety of apple has its own special conditions for maximum storage life. The Bramley Seedling variety requires about 10 per cent carbon dioxide, with a corresponding drop in the oxygen content. This composition of the atmosphere can be achieved by the natural respiration of the fruit in the unventilated chamber, and maintained by controlled ventilation when the required mixture has been reached. The

Cox's Orange Pippin variety will not store well with more than 5 per cent carbon dioxide and 2.5 per cent oxygen. To reduce the oxygen to this level without allowing the carbon dioxide to build up beyond 5 per cent, the atmosphere of the storage chamber must be circulated through a scrubber, which takes out the excess carbon dioxide. This method of storage enables this very important variety to be kept in good condition until May. From January to May there is a serious gap in the supply of home-grown fruit to the British market, which the satisfactory storage of apples has done much to close.

Just as the cold storage of apples involves the study of each individual variety, so in the freezing of fruit and vegetables no two products can be handled in an identical way. Nearly all vegetables have to be scalded before they are frozen, if they are not to become flabby when they are thawed out. Fruits like strawberries, raspberries, and black currants require no heat treatment before freezing but others, like cherries and plums, turn brown on thawing unless they are scalded or protected with a syrup containing citric or ascorbic acid.

The explanation of why all these variations in technique are required is still far from complete; much of what we do is still empirical. Extensive research is, however, answering many questions, so that each year the work can be undertaken with greater certainty and the product reaching the housewife steadily improved.

When we speak of dehydration as a means of preservation, we mean no more than drying — the oldest form of food preservation — by artificial means, usually a combination of heating and low humidity. The first attempts at dehydration arose from the need to supply troops in the field with rations of small bulk and weight. The obvious way to achieve this is to remove the water in such a way that it can be replaced and the food reconstituted. The American Civil War and the Boer War saw attempts to dehydrate vegetables; they met with little success.

In World War I large quantities of dehydrated vegetables were supplied to the United States Navy, with very mixed results. Some, it is recorded, were at least edible, but a large part went straight overboard. The variation in the sailors' reactions was probably due to the introduction by some firms of scalding before dehydration. Even the best efforts, however, were not such as to make dehydrated foods as acceptable as those preserved by other means. There were a few dehydrated products in general use in the years between the wars, notably dried milk and fruits, but it was not until World War II that any major advance was made. Once more the need was great, and in England the food research station in Cambridge was set to work on the problem, with instructions to cooperate as fully as possible with research in the laboratories of the Allies. These joint investigations provided much of the knowledge which was required by the scientists in industry and the Ministry of Food, and by 1941 many dehydrated foods were playing a major part in the war effort. It was shown, for example, that foods containing fats tend to go rancid if they are too dry and store best if they have a moisture content of about 10 per cent, while non-fatty foods store best when the moisture content is as low as possible. The need for nitrogen-filled, air-tight packages was demonstrated if the period of storage was to be prolonged and the carotene and ascorbic acid contents preserved.

In spite of these advances in technique, however, dehydrated foods were regarded as suitable only for emergencies. Thankful as the British housewife had been for dehydrated eggs and potatoes during the war, she was only too glad to return to fresh food and food stored and preserved by other means when peace came. As so often happens, research which had been directed to the improvement of an old and well-known technique indicated a new approach to the problem. In the last ten years, a new dehydration process has been developed which is essentially similar to the "freeze-drying" used in the laboratory for storing microbial cultures. So far, this method of storage has been used only on a limited commercial scale, but the products from pilot plants have been shown to be excellent. It is possible to dehydrate a steak and reconstitute it so that in physical form, chemical composition, and flavor it is indistinguishable from the fresh meat. In years to come, this means of preservation may well become a serious competitor with the other well-established techniques.

Many foods can be stored without any special treatment. Grain, if it is sufficiently dry, will keep for long periods in silos. Potatoes and other root crops can be stored for many months in the field covered with earth. Storage in these forms presents a series of special problems. With grain, the chief difficulty is to protect it from insect and animal pests. The loss of grain from attacks by rodents and insects in the less developed countries is very high, estimates place it between one-third and one-half. Grain can be protected from rodents by storage in silos or bins which prevent access. Protection against insect pests is much more difficult and requires chemical fumigation in closed containers. Attempts have been made to use high-energy sources of gamma rays to kill grain weevils and flour moths. The results have been scientifically successful, the insects being killed without damage to the grain, but so far the technique has not been applied successfully on a commercial scale. The present cost of installing and operating a high-energy source renders the method more expensive than the conventional use of fumigants. With the development of cheaper and more easily managed high-energy sources, however, this use of radioactivity may prove to be of great value in protecting grain stored in bulk.

Potatoes stored without treatment begin to sprout and become flabby and finally inedible. When the stores are opened there is always wastage, and various chemical treatments have been used to prevent sprouting. There is objection to this method, because the chemicals used may be toxic. Exposure of potatoes to a moderately large dose of gamma rays, about one-fourth of that needed to destroy insects, prevents sprouting. Here again, the problem is one of devising a cheap means of treating the potatoes. Clearly a source of the type needed cannot be carted around the farms, so the potatoes must be taken to a central store; this is an expensive operation, and so far the loss of potatoes stored in the field is less costly than the treatment. Where, however, potatoes are normally stored in a central building this technique may prove to be valuable.

To no group of scientists does man owe a greater debt than to that which has, over the years, devised means for storing and preserving food; yet no other group has been so often vilified. Without the efforts of these scientists it is impossible to imagine how life in our great modern cities could exist; serious as the food situation is in our world of rapidly expanding populations, it would already have reached famine proportions if food were not being protected in storehouses and preserved by the many efficient processes now available. The public forgets all the debts they owe and remembers only the failures, most of which have resulted from a desire to help too quickly before the process has been fully proved. For the future, the food scientist should keep in mind that only good food will be good when it has been preserved — he cannot make a silk purse out of a sow's ear — and that he should never launch a new product on a skeptical world until he is doubly sure of its safety, its nutritive value, and its palatability.

This is particularly true of any process involving the use of a radioactive source. The layman, because he is aware of danger from nuclear fall-out from atomic explosions, has acquired an irrational fear of the effects of nuclear radiation, and hence he will be only too ready to blame food treated in this way for any ills he may suffer, whether or not there is any evidence to justify his fears.

# 4

# THE DEVELOPING COUNTRIES

A LL COUNTRIES are developing; any which are not are moribund. It is, therefore, right to speak of more developed and the less developed countries, rather than to single out one group of countries as underdeveloped. Any such designation suggests a difference in fundamental character rather than what is, in fact, a difference in the stage reached in education and in the application of science and technology to agriculture and industry.

As a consequence of lack of education and low standard of living, the less-developed countries are, as a whole, overpopulated, some grossly so — a condition which becomes worse each day owing to a high birth rate and an increasing expectation of life. Common humanity demands that the more highly developed countries should give medical aid to the less developed in which disease and malnutrition have taken and are taking a heavy toll, particularly among young children. Yet in doing so they are making worse many of the problems which face these countries. Each new mouth to be fed swallows up some of the resources which are sorely needed if the rate of development is to be maintained, let alone increased.

The shortage of resources for development is another factor common to almost all the less developed countries. As a group, they have been the suppliers of food and raw materials to the countries with highly developed manufacturing industries, buying in return the products of the factories. The resulting economy provided little or no surplus for cultural or industrial progress. Economic expansion is like those chemical reactions which require a certain input of energy before they begin, but, once begun, generate the energy necessary for their ever increasing expansion. If nothing is done to help the less developed countries with their economy, if there is no input of energy from without, the gap between them and the more developed countries will continue to widen.

There are factors other than rising populations and lack of available funds which have tended to enlarge this gap. The major part of the less developed area of the world lies in tropical or subtropical regions. Here heat and disease sap the vitality of the people in a way that those living in more temperate climates cannot easily understand. Rainfall tends to be insufficient, highly seasonal, or excessive. In areas where it is insufficient, the land is barren desert; where it is highly seasonal there is alternate flood and drought; where it is excessive the rain forest presses down like a great octopus threatening to strangle man's feeble efforts to cultivate the land.

In desert lands crops can be grown only if they can be irrigated; to do this heavy capital expenditure on dams and canals is involved. Without irrigation the economy must rest on a nomadic agriculture, cattle, sheep, and goats being driven where any sparse vegetation and water are to be found.

Although in countries of seasonal rains good crops can be grown, there are grave limitations. The time of planting is limited by the period of the rains. Nothing can be done, other than the preparation of the land, until the rains come. Then all the sowing must be completed quickly, so that the seed has germinated and the young plants have become so well rooted that they will continue to grow through the period of drought. If the rains are late or poor there may be complete crop failure of a kind unknown in temperate climates. The demands on farm labor in these countries are periodic. The farmer may have to sit waiting days or weeks for the rains; then for a short while he must work all the hours he can, only to wait again until his crops come to harvest. The effective full employment of labor under these conditions presents grave problems, particularly when any large-scale farming is attempted.

In the lands of heavy rains the first and ever present problem is to clear the land of forest for cropping and to keep it clear. When this has to be done by hand it is a heavy task, with the inevitable result that the farmer tries to manage with the minimum of land.

A traditional system of farming in these areas is to clear a small patch of bush, burning as much as possible and incorporating the ash in the soil. This land is then cropped continuously until the joint action of the crops and the leaching of the heavy rains removes the stored nutrients, and yields begin to fall. Another patch of bush is then cleared, and the worn-out land is allowed to go back to forest. Such a system calls for a large area of land for each peasant cultivator, and as population increases, the time the land can be rested under the bush fallow has to be shorter. In the end there can be no bush fallow, and the land must be kept under continuous cultivation. When this stage is reached, crops can be grown only by the generous use of purchased fertilizers, the cost of which the peasant, with little or no cash, cannot afford. He must then be helped to maintain the fertility of his land until means can be found whereby he can earn enough, either from cash crops or by some industrial activity, to do so himself.

In tropical and subtropical countries, farm livestock are subject to many devastating diseases. Only by the exercise of the most careful control measures can these be contained. Moreover, for a variety of religious and social reasons the number of animals exceeds the keep available. As a result, large herds of undernourished and diseased animals consume food without providing either meat or milk, and serve as a reservoir of disease from which any healthy stock is infected.

The people of these countries also have to contend with the climate. In the drier climates there are intense heat, dust, and flies; in the wetter climates, heat, high humidity, and almost every kind of biting insect, many of them carrying disease. In temperate climates, we may have periods of heat and high humidity and periods of intense cold, but we have the spring and fall, and we have learned to heat our houses against the cold and to condition them against the heat.

The people in the less developed countries have none of these amenities, nor, in general, have they piped water supplies or proper systems of sanitation. They are enervated by the heat and humidity; they are subject to endemic tropical diseases, many of which do not kill but sap the energy of the sufferer; and by and large they have a diet which is unbalanced and inadequate.

If these countries are to progress, they must have help not only in growing better crops but also in managing their livestock and in providing better living conditions for themselves. It is vital, however, that this help be given in a form which they are prepared to accept. Religious observance, social attitudes, traditions, and taboos must be respected and overcome; there must be no suggestion of patronage; and remedies must be practical in the light of existing circumstances. To achieve these ends a system of broadly based education is essential, and advisers must be found from outside who are not only technically expert but who know, understand, and sympathize with the people.

Although the less developed countries have many characteristics in common there are marked regional differences. There are four main regions where development is retarded: Central Africa, parts of the Mediterranean seaboard and the Middle East, the Far East, and parts of the South American continent.

In the Far East many of the countries have a history and culture older than any in Western Europe, but for a variety of reasons — religious, cultural, political, and climatic — they took little part in the industrial revolution of the nineteenth century, based as it was on the discoveries of modern science. Asia is also the area of greatest population pressure: In 1951 there was only two-thirds of an acre of arable land for each of its estimated 1,637,000,000 people. Great efforts are now being made to increase the available arable land. In the last decade 220,000,000 acres, or roughly 25 per cent, was added, but this large area only served to provide the same two-thirds of an acre for the 353,000,000 rise in population, also roughly 25 per cent. New land is not inexhaustible and cannot continue to be brought under cultivation at this rate. Moreover, the new land will, with each advance, be more and more hardly won as less promising areas are attacked.

There are only two solutions to the Asian problem. In the long run the population must be limited. Modern medicine has increased the expectation of life in these countries, and in particular it has reduced the infant mortality. Unless the number of births can be reduced, the population of Asia must reach a point where it will burst its bounds and flood over other parts of the world, many themselves already overpopulated. The governments of most of the Asian countries are only too well aware of the enormous problem which is facing them and are taking steps to introduce means of population control. But they are handicapped by the general low standard of education and of living. It is in countries with a broadly based educational system and a high standard of living that voluntary family limitation is widely accepted.

While governments struggle with this long-term problem, the population will continue to increase, and a short-term solution is needed to meet the rapidly rising demand for food.

In these Asian countries food production is still in the hands of peasants, each cultivating his one-man holding. The only large-scale farming is concerned with plantation crops for export, such as tea, coffee, palm oil, and rubber. The peasants are shrewd but illiterate and suspicious of change. They live in largely self-contained villages with few wants other than those which the village supplies, and they send to the towns and cities only the food they do not need for their own use, unless they are forced to do otherwise. The level of production on their holdings is low and will remain so until they see good reason for raising it. Yields could be increased easily and rapidly by the use of the right fertilizers, but this involves the expenditure of money which the peasant does not have. Means must be found to provide him with the first quantities of fertilizer, to show him how to use them, and then to insure him a market which will give him an adequate return, paying for the fertilizers and leaving something to compensate him for the extra work and risk involved.

Fertilizers are of no use without adequate water supplies, so in the more arid areas the crops must be irrigated; until this can be done the yields cannot be raised. Where both water and fertilizers are available and heavier crops grown they must be protected against pests, diseases, and damage from wild animals. These peasant holdings are on the whole unsuited for the use of chemical sprays for insect and disease control. Not only does this involve a further expenditure of money on the growing crop, but in the hands of men who have no experience with materials of this kind they may be dangerous. If, however, there is no other way, they must be used; but efforts should first be made to protect the crop by the provision of resistant varieties and by sound cultural practices.

Wild animals, particularly monkeys, cause extensive damage to crops in many parts of Asia. If money and labor are to be spent on growing heavier crops, some way must be found to control these animals and the harvested crops must be protected during storage and marketing. The losses at this stage are enormous, and their elimination alone would go a long way toward raising the diet of an undernourished people to an adequate level.

It has been estimated that for every really hungry man in the world there are probably five suffering from malnutrition. In the East the number must be much higher, for only the wealthier enjoy a reasonably balanced diet. Where there is an adequate intake of calories, there are still shortages of good-quality protein and certain of the essential vitamins. These can be added to the diet in the form of animal products, principally meat, eggs, and milk. The task of providing these necessary items of diet is greatly increased in many parts of Asia by religious and sociological difficulties. Where the cow is held to be a sacred animal it cannot be slaughtered, much less eaten. As a result, there is a vast cattle population consuming fodder but so underfed that it produces little or no human food. For a large part of the population of the East the flesh of the pig, one of the most efficient sources of protein and fat, is forbidden. Ways and means are being found of overcoming these difficulties, but they are slow and so far only touch the fringes of the problem.

The area comprising the Middle East and Mediterranean coastal regions is similar in many ways to the Far East. It, too, has an old civilization. Many of its great empires had achieved a high level of culture when Western Europe was still a land of barbarians, but these empires passed; and while the temperate zones of Europe, under the unifying influence of Christendom, moved forward through the Renaissance to the scientific developments of the seventeenth and eighteenth centuries and finally to the industrial revolution of the nineteenth, they became fragmented into small states based on an unchanged peasant agriculture, in large part nomadic in character. As the result of disease and almost continuous warfare, their populations showed no great increase and the standard of living and education of the mass of the people remained low.

With the improvement of the means of transport and the onset of the industrial revolution, trade began to flow more freely, the countries of Western Europe sending manufactured goods in return for food and raw materials. Western ideas, too, began to reach not only the cosmopolitan wealthy, but also the mass of the people.

The period between the two world wars brought great changes in this area which have been further accelerated during the last decade. Countries which had been dependencies have claimed their independence, and all are endeavoring to develop toward Western standards. There has been a great liberalizing movement, not only in politics but also in social conditions. Populations have begun to rise rapidly; that of Turkey, for example, has doubled since 1920. The cities and towns have grown quickly, drawing in the excess population, but the agriculture has changed little. It is still predominantly an area of small peasant farmers and nomadic herdsmen. The agricultural output has shown no marked increase and is not meeting the needs of the growing population. The one notable exception in this area is Israel, where the injection of large amounts of capital from Jewish communities throughout the world, and the trained skill and devotion of those who have gone to Israel from many lands, have created a flourishing farm system, and a rapidly developing manufacturing industry. Many of the countries in the area have neither the wealth nor the skill to achieve comparable results. What wealth there is — and those countries with revenues from oil have great wealth — is ill-distributed, both among countries and within each country. Modern cities are springing up alongside the old, where blocks of flats, large public buildings, luxury hotels, and shopping streets crowded with modern cars serve a growing bureaucracy and trading community, while life for the peasant changes little or not at all. Many of these countries can no longer feed themselves, and where they have no surplus income from exports such as oil they are dependent on the generosity of the United States for their bread. The old universities are growing rapidly in size and new ones are being founded, but this is only touching the fringe of the people, a fringe drawn mostly from the towns and cities.

While basic elementary education expands only slowly, and the great problem of illiteracy remains virtually untouched, industry is being developed to save exchange on imported manufactured products. So far as this provides the basic materials and machines for agriculture or makes funds available for purchasing food, it is all to the good. If, however, it is directed to the production of consumer goods for the towns and cities, while investment in agriculture is neglected and reliance is placed on the continuing generosity of the countries with farming surpluses, it can only tend to increase the present unstable position.

Central Africa differs in many ways from Asia and the Middle Eastern and Mediterranean areas. Unlike them, it has no ancient civilization or culture. Except for some of the West Coast ports, equatorial Africa was largely unknown to the world until the nineteenth century. The Arab slave traders had routes across the deserts of the north, but these gave no cultural contact between the outside world and the African tribes. Scholars at the new universities of Central Africa are trying to piece together the history of this great region, but they are finding many difficulties owing to the lack of any written records. It was not until missionaries came from Europe that the tribal languages were set down in writing for the translation of the Bible. They also started elementary and later secondary schools which have been expanded by the colonial governments. Many of the African political leaders owe their education to the early mission schools. As a result, the degree of literacy is much higher in many Central African countries than in Asia or the Middle East.

The area is potentially rich, but its wealth has to be hard-won. The climate, over a large part, has to be fought. The arid regions often change rapidly into those of intense rainfall. Even where the rainfall is moderate it is markedly seasonal, and from time to time it fails completely, with disastrous results. In many parts of the region, debilitating diseases of man and animals are endemic, although modern preventive medicine, both human and veterinary, is doing much to reduce their incidence.

Distances in Africa are great and the terrain is difficult for rail and road transport. Long stretches of railway and of roads have to be maintained, often through barren and unproductive country, to provide for the transport of cash crops, and the mineral wealth of the interior to the coast for export.

Intertribal warfare, famine, and disease have in the past prevented any rapid rise in population. With the arrival of the colonial powers these checks on population growth have been slowly removed.

It is not often realized for how short a time the white man has had any major influence in Central Africa. Trade with the West Coast is of old standing, much of it sullied in the past by traffic in slaves, but up to the time of World War I it was still known as the "White Man's Grave," and few Europeans lived far from the coastal towns. In the east, too, the white man was largely confined to the coastal towns, until the railways opened up the rich countries in Central Africa at the beginning of the twentieth century. Before the coming of the railways the only means of transport was on foot, with native porters carrying all that was needed for the journey and often cutting a way through dense undergrowth. There are men only recently retired from the British colonial services who began their careers as District Officers by making a journey of hundreds of miles in this way to the place to which they had been posted. Once they reached their station, their most rapid means of communication with the outside world was often a native runner.

Following the railways, development was rapid; the growing of such cash crops as coffee, cotton, and tobacco, the ranching of cattle, and the mining of great mineral wealth brought in European settlers and Indian traders. At the same time, stable governments were set up which prevented tribal warfare, began the control of disease, and through their steadily growing wealth provided the means of combating famine.

Parallel with the development in East and Central Africa, disease control and the construction of roads were opening up the interior of the West Coast countries. Here, too, there was mineral wealth, but there were also exportable crops such as cocoa, palm oils, and ground nuts which were very suitable for cultivation by African farmers. Partly because from the first the African population could produce export crops and partly because of the climate, there were few settlers in West Africa. Europeans who went there were primarily administrators, technical experts, and traders.

Between the two world wars, the countries of Africa grew in wealth, the primary education developed, and secondary and university education made a beginning. The medical services began the gigantic task of dealing with endemic disease, and agricultural and veterinary advisers were helping to raise the standard of African native farming and of the plantation crops. Inevitably, with these changes the population began to rise and in some areas a land shortage developed. Apart from the times of crop failure, there was little actual hunger, but there was chronic widespread malnutrition. African diets all tend to lack high-quality protein, which can only be supplied by meat, milk, eggs, and fish. There are many natural difficulties in the way of the stock farmer, but these can be and are being overcome in the Central African countries by the control of disease and the introduction of better farming systems.

There are, however, sociological problems which present even greater difficulties. Over a large part of the region, cattle are the accepted currency and each cow counts as one, whether it is a diseased bag of bones or a healthy, well-nourished animal. As a result, no one wishes to slaughter a poor animal any more than we should wish to burn a dollar bill or a pound note because it was torn and dirty. These "currency" cattle have to be fed to live, but there is often only enough pasture and other feed to keep them alive and not enough to make them reasonably productive animals. The African farmer is gradually beginning to trust other forms of money; the more wealthy have begun to use banks. If this process can continue and the number of cattle be materially reduced, there is every hope that the output of good animal protein can be increased. There still remains the problem of persuading the African to introduce adequate quantities into his regular diet. Tradition is difficult to overcome, and in some countries of Central Africa there are definite taboos against the eating of some forms of animal protein. Thus, in Uganda it is believed that eating eggs will render a woman sterile: yet this is one of the easiest and cheapest forms of protein to produce. Until tradition and superstition can be overcome, malnutrition will continue to apply a brake to development. Not only must education open the way to still better food production, but it must at the same time create a proper understanding of the value of a more balanced diet and so establish a demand for what the more enlightened farmers produce.

It is virtually impossible to write in general terms of the less developed countries of the vast continent of South America. There are great differences in their natural wealth; not only in their total potential wealth, but also in the form this takes and the degree of difficulty involved in its exploitation. Within each country, too, there is great disparity in the distribution of wealth. South America has some of the world's most magnificent modern cities; they grow at a great pace and with their ancillary services are absorbing the major part of capital available for development. South America also has a great part of the world's undeveloped land suitable for food production, and much of that already in use could be made to yield far more by more intensive management. Some of these countries have been food exporters on a major scale, and still do export but in smaller quantities. It is doubtful whether, with more than one or two exceptions, their present food production is sufficient to give their growing populations an adequately balanced diet. Even in the wealthier countries, although there may be no positive hunger there is the malnutrition of ignorance and poverty. These countries should be able to finance their own development, with the aid of private capital investment from the more developed countries. Foreign capital will be directed for the most part to industrial development; the money required for the opening-up of more land for food production will have to come from their own resources. This will involve a redirection of effort from the development of cities to the development of villages and the land. It must also mean some redistribution of wealth if those who need the additional food produced are to have the money to buy it.

The poorer countries will not be able to finance rural development from their own resources and will require help from other than private investors. Apart from this need, their problems are similar — a growing population, an unequal distribution of wealth, and an emphasis on industrial and urban development at the expense of agriculture and food production. These factors are among the basic causes of the political instability of the continent.

The more developed areas of the world are willing and anxious to help the less developed, partly from purely altruistic motives and partly from self-interest. They realize that the world can never be truly at peace while per capita income in the less developed countries is less than one-twentieth of that in the United States or one-tenth of that in the United Kingdom; while, in a world in which there is an over-all shortage of food, many of the more developed countries have a surplus the less developed cannot buy; and while, although the more advanced countries move steadily forward to higher standards of education, more than half the world's population remains illiterate. They realize too that, in spite of all that has been done, these disparities are not lessening but are rather growing because of the greater population increase in the less developed countries, an increase which is absorbing any rise achieved in food production and any increase in national income, so that the individual is no better fed and has no more material wealth, and the nation as a whole has no more margin for capital investment.

We must now ask ourselves what can be done to right this chronic ill-balance and what science can do to help. The task of raising the standard of living in these countries must rest on their governments. The more developed countries can help with money, materials, and expert knowledge, but the individual plan and its execution for each country must be the work of its own leaders. It is only they who can command the necessary response from the people.

Clearly, the one major necessity is to limit the population increase. In man, as in all animals, survival in a primitive world requires a potentially high rate of reproduction in order to meet the losses from famine, disease, and the attacks of other men and animals. By his skill in medicine man has greatly reduced the losses from disease, and by his farming skill and his ability to transport food across the world he has materially cut down losses from famine. Although he still finds it necessary to indulge from time to time in the slaughter of a world war, he has developed a social conscience, which has largely eliminated the continuous killings of tribal wars and private vendettas, and his possession of superior weapons has done away with the risk of attack from wild animals. At the same time his individual reproductive capacity has increased, owing to his longer life span. Unless we limit this reproductive capacity, our numbers must continue to rise at an ever increasing rate until the world can no longer hold us. In the more developed countries, the rise in numbers has already been checked; in the years from 1951 to 1959 the population of Europe rose by only 6.3 per cent compared with 27 per cent in Asia and 21 per cent in Africa. This lower reproductive rate has been linked with universal education and a higher standard of living for the mass of people; the one has given them the intellectual capacity needed to limit their families, the other the will to do so in order to maintain the steady rise in their material well-being. It is reasonable to expect that better education and a high standard of living would have a similar effect on the rate of reproduction in the less developed countries. The rate at which a reduction in birth rate can be achieved in these countries could, however, be accelerated if science were to evolve a simpler method of contraception, particularly if it were one to which there were no serious social or religious objections.

To achieve a standard where reproductive capacity is checked, those responsible for the government of the less developed countries must aim to expand education at a rate which will outstrip the growing population. This is a formidable task, and one which can only be accomplished if help is forthcoming from outside, both in the supply of skilled teachers and in money. The provision of high-school and university education is difficult enough, but it is relatively easy compared to the provision of elementary education for the millions. Thousands of small schools must be built and teachers found for them from among the educated youth whose ambitions are, not unnaturally, directed toward a glamorous future in the cities rather than to the unspectacular life of a village schoolmaster.

Parallel to a rise in educational standards there must be a growth in national wealth, which will not only maintain but permit a steady increase in the standard of living as the number among which it has to be divided grows. The leaders in these countries have many difficult choices to make. The first and most difficult is to decide how much of the national income, together with funds coming from without, should be used to provide capital for the expansion of the productive capacity of the country and how much should be distributed to raise the immediate standard of living of the people. The next question is in what way this standard should be raised. Once the mass of people have more money to spend they must be provided with food and manufactured goods they can buy.

Here enters a dangerous desire to provide evidence of progress by setting up factories for making goods of the type sought after by workers in the countries of high individual incomes, where the basic necessities of food and clothing are already available in plenty. Automobiles, labor-saving appliances in the home, and many luxury articles will find a market in the towns and cities and create a demand for higher incomes there, but they will leave untouched the greater part of the people, in particular the peasant population on which a better food supply must depend. To the superficial observer, seeing only the cosmopolitan centers of the big cities, the presence of first-class hotels, large modern buildings, wide streets crowded with motor traffic, and shops displaying a wide variety of consumer goods may suggest rapid progress and a justification for financial support in gifts and loans. Yet this apparent prosperity may in fact be a retrograde step, in that it is absorbing money which should be spent on raising the basic standard of all the people, in providing more food so that men are no longer hungry or undernourished, and in making simple clothes and homes available to all. At the same time it is increasing the disparity between the relative wealth of the towns and poverty of the rural population.

To the politician, often dependent for his power on the better educated and richer townspeople, it is a difficult choice. If he follows the right way and puts the funds at his disposal into the improvement of agriculture, the manufacture or purchase of fertilizers and farm equipment, and the production of goods that the peasant wishes to buy, he may find himself out of office; if he caters to the townsman's wants and provides him with the means to procure them, he will be creating an unstable economy, dependent on continuous support from without. Should that support be withdrawn or fail to match the growing demands, he may find himself with a revolution on his hands and be lucky to escape with his life.

In nothing is this dilemma more clearly seen than in the application of science to the problems of the less developed countries. What these countries need more than anything else are men, trained and willing to solve the many problems involved in the improvement of agricultural practice and ready to go out into the fields to instruct the farmers and help them put to use the technical knowledge which will raise production. Much of this, however, is unspectacular work; often it is no more than the adaptation to local conditions of practices well established elsewhere.

Every less developed country feels that to prove its advancing status it must have laboratories carrying out research in the fields where the boundaries of scientific knowledge are being rapidly pushed ahead, and that means first and foremost nuclear physics. In many of the less developed countries today, the one really well-equipped laboratory is that in which nuclear physics is being studied. The science schools of the universities may be starved for equipment, the laboratories serving agriculture may be few and lack many of the bare essentials for research, yet the atomic physics laboratories often challenge those in the more developed countries in their lavish and expensive apparatus and equipment. The men in these laboratories, trained as most have been in the United States and Europe, are often working on problems of the most fundamental character, far removed from the pressing needs of their own country. It is not surprising that many of the best brains among the students are drawn to atomic physics and help to swell the spurious impression that nuclear science is the basis on which their future prosperity is to be built.

There is, however, a way open by which this natural desire to work in the exciting field of nuclear physics can, to some degree, be harnessed to the immediate needs of agriculture. It lies in the use which can be made of radioactive isotopes to solve agricultural and veterinary problems. The work of the CENTO Institute of Nuclear Science in Tehran serves as a good example of the way in which interest in nuclear science can be channeled toward the problems of importance in the Middle East.

This Institute was set up in the first place as a center for training scientists from the CENTO countries, Turkey, Iran, and Pakistan, in the techniques required for research in the field of nuclear physics. It did useful work in this way, but its functions have been gradually changed so that it is now devoted to the study of the uses which can be made of radioactive isotopes in solving problems of importance in the general development of the region. It does this in two ways: Scientists go to the Institute for postgraduate training, during which they work on a problem involving the use of radioactive substances in the field of science which they propose to follow in their future careers. They are then in a position to make use of tracer techniques in their future research, when this offers the best method of solving the problem they are attacking. Its second function is to help scientists working in the CENTO countries who are already qualified to carry out research but who wish to use radioactive isotopes in their work. This involves sending men from the Institute to study the problem on the spot, to advise on the technique to be used, and, if necessary, to help in the design of special equipment which can if necessary be built in the Institute. It may also be possible to bring about collaboration between, for example, someone working in one of the biological sciences and a fellow countryman working in the nuclear physics laboratory, a collaboration which could help to direct the attention of nuclear physicists to problems of immediate national importance.

Workers at the Institute are studying a wide range of problems and using many different radioactive isotopes. Sodium-22 is being used in studies of salinity. Plants labeled with phosphorus-32 are enabling research workers to follow the feeding habits of aphids. Labeling with iodine-131 is being tried as a means of measuring the efficiency of a ghanat — the ancient irrigation tunnel of Iran, on which the country still relies for water supplies. The flight range of the mosquito is being measured by labeling with phosphorus-32. Tantalum-182 wire is being used to study the underground movement of plague rats.

These are a few examples selected at random from a list of nearly fifty projects covering the fields of agriculture, hydrology, and medicine. There is no longer any call from the CENTO countries for help in training or research in nuclear physics; they already have or will soon have their own reactors and many trained physicists. Now, having satisfied their desire to be in the forefront of fashionable research, they are turning to the study of problems of major importance to their own economy, but it will not be easy to attract the right men into this work unless it appears to have some relationship to nuclear physics, which next to space research is the most powerful means of extracting funds from national and international sources.

Although one must regret the undue emphasis on nuclear physics in the less developed countries which can ill afford to duplicate fundamental research being done elsewhere, some return may well be obtained on the heavy initial outlay in the fields of radio-medicine, radio-agriculture, and use of radioactive tracers for the solutions of problems arising in hydrology and in the newly developing industries. Let us hope this will prove so.

The less developed countries now hold a key position in world affairs. In each there is a continuing struggle between the ideals of democratic freedom and those of communism. Any breakdown of government, with resulting chaos, provides the agitator with the opportunity he needs to sow the seeds of communism.

If we wish to defend the ideals for which the Western countries stand, we must help these countries to evolve a sound basic economy, but the time for unquestioning charity is past. The wealthier, more developed countries have so far tended to treat the less developed as we as individuals would treat an impecunious friend. We have given money and goods when they have been asked, without, from fear of hurting our friend's feelings, inquiring too closely into the wisdom of his subsequent actions. When, however, the demands continue to come at regular intervals and tend to rise each time, until our own resources are strained, a point is reached when prudence demands an inquiry into the basic cause of the trouble and an attempt to direct further help to remedying the fault.

It has been easy to argue that the less developed countries are independent and masters of their own destiny and hence that they should be allowed to spend the aid they are given very much as they wish. If they decide to embark on expensive research in nuclear physics rather than on research affecting their agricultural economy, who are we to say no?

Moreover, unconditional help is easy to give in that it involves only writing a check. To sit down with those we are helping, and to work out with them the effects of different courses of action open to them in spending what we can afford to give, calls for a gift of time and effort. But it is the only way of achieving lasting goodwill between the giver and the receiver. Indiscriminate charity, creating as it does the impression of a bottomless purse, results in wasteful spending. When the purse proves to be empty, many essential things will still remain undone, things which have been set aside for unimportant but desirable objectives. The recipient then is angry at seeing his plans wrecked for lack of money and turns his anger against his benefactor, blaming him because he has no more to give.

This is a story as old as the world, but we have to learn it afresh each time we help a friend. Let us learn in time to give help to the poorer countries with discretion, so that the maximum return may come from this help not only in material things but, more important still, in the creation of goodwill among the peoples of the world.

# 5

# FALL-OUT AND FOOD CHAINS

**F**EW SUBJECTS have been more discussed or have caused more controversy than the effect on mankind of fall-out from nuclear tests. That there has been an increase in the radioactivity to which we are all exposed is beyond question. All thinking people are rightly concerned about its effects, particularly on young children, and are seeking authoritative information. Yet there can be few questions on which scientific opinion has varied so widely. At one extreme, the scientist usually concerned with nuclear testing is ready to make soothing optimistic statements, dismissing the risk as negligible; at the other, the scientist emotionally involved in the controversy over the use of nuclear weapons issues alarmingly pessimistic statements claiming that before long a large part of the population will be suffering from leukemia and that there will be many genetic abnormalities in the newborn. They are of course both wrong, as scientists are when they cease to be objective and let their personal desires and fears cloud their judgment. The truth lies somewhere between these two extremes.

The great difficulty with which scientists were faced, when radioactivity began to rise as the result of nuclear explosions, was that there was far too little concrete evidence on which to base answers to the many urgent questions asked by the ordinary man and woman. In order to satisfy the demand for guidance, all the scientist could do was to speculate on the basis of the little evidence he had, with the inevitable result that his conclusions were sometimes colored by his own feelings.

Over the past decade, much new experimental evidence has been obtained on the way in which radioactive fall-out enters into the food chain, how this affects the radioactive content of the diet of different groups, and the resulting exposure of individuals to different types of radiation. There still remains the medical question of the consequences of this exposure which, because of the probable long-term effects and the low levels of radiation involved, is most difficult to answer. It is not within the scope of this book to consider the medical aspects of the problem; that was most ably done a year ago by Dr. Loutit.[1] Where at any time it may be necessary to compare levels of contamination with those regarded as a danger to health, the figures accepted by international medical authorities should be used.

The man or woman, and particularly the woman with young children, who has no special scientific knowledge is demanding answers to a number of questions. "How real is the danger from radioactive fall-out? Is this danger more nearly related to the fall-out from recent explosions, or is there a cumulative effect depending on the total fall-out? So far as there is a danger from fall-out, is there anything I can do to protect myself and my family from it? Should I, for example, be wise to cut out certain items from my normal diet?"

Clearly the answers to these questions must differ for almost every family group. Generalizations can be made for those in the same country, in the same income group, and with the same dietary habits, but even within such a restricted sample of population, individual preferences may materially affect the intake of radioactive material.

Some simple knowledge, however, of the way radioactive nu-

[1] John F. Loutit, *Irradiation of Mice and Men* (Chicago: University of Chicago Press, 1962).

clides are taken up in the food chain, of how these are distributed among the different components of diet, and of their fate when they are ingested by man will help to assess the true danger to the individual arising from different kinds and levels of fall-out.

It will also help to prevent the taking of unnecessary steps to avoid unimportant risks from fall-out, which in themselves create other and graver dangers to health. How easily this can happen was shown some few years ago in part of Wales. Higher than average values for strontium-90 were claimed for samples of herbage on which cattle were grazing. It was erroneously assumed by the local people that, as a result, drinking the milk produced by local herds constituted a real danger to children. Mothers, fearful of the consequences, began to withhold milk from their children's diets. If the mistaken impression had not been corrected, very serious dietary deficiencies would have resulted.

In a single lecture it is not possible to deal with all aspects of this complex subject. What follows, therefore, is no more than a brief summary. It has been necessary to make a number of generalizations, omitting many qualifications which would be proper in a detailed discussion. These generalizations are based on the best evidence available to me.

It is fortunately not necessary, in order to assess the danger from fall-out, to take into account a wide range of radioactive fission products; we need consider only those which are produced in quantity during an explosion, which have a moderate to long half-life, and whose chemical and biological characteristics are such that they are first taken into the food chain and then absorbed by man when the food is eaten. There are four fission products which fulfill these conditions; they are iodine-131, cesium-137, and the two isotopes of strontium, -89 and -90.[2] The four nuclides we are considering fall into two groups,

[2] Although carbon-14 is estimated to produce the same amount of total harm as strontium-90, because of its half-life of 5,600 years its effect will

iodine-131 and strontium-89 with relatively short half-lives measured in days, and cesium-137 and strontium-90 with half-lives of 37 and 28 years, respectively. Clearly, iodine-131 and strontium-89 present only a passing danger, and unless they are absorbed rapidly in the food chain and the food quickly eaten by man, they will have no effect. Any damage they do must be done quickly and as a result of high concentrations.

With their long half-lives, cesium-137 and strontium-90 do not necessarily have to be absorbed quickly in the food chain; they could remain in the soil for years and under favorable conditions still be available to the plant and hence find their way into human diet. It is important, therefore, in considering these nuclides to take into account their fate in the soil and how far any build-up in the soil is available to the plants growing on it.

It is these fission products, too, which are capable, if they are ingested and retained in the human body, of causing damage over a long period.

Iodine, cesium, and strontium each have their own chemical characteristics. Each is taken up in different ways by plants, each is absorbed at different rates from the intestinal tract of animals, and each has a different distribution within the animal organism. It is necessary to take into account all these characteristics, in assessing the amounts of the different nuclides contained in the fall-out reaching the earth's surface which will find their way into the different parts of the human body.

We can determine the quantities of the different fission products present in any given sample of an individual item of diet, but the information so obtained must be examined with caution. First, it is essential that the sample should be correctly drawn, so that it is as representative as possible of the bulk of the foodstuff. It is also essential to know the content of other elements similar in chemical character to the fission product which

be spread over more than 10,000 years, as compared with one generation for strontium-90. It can, therefore, be omitted from our present considerations.

influence first its adsorption by the intestine and then its distribution in the body tissues.

With knowledge of the amounts of radioactive fission products in the individual items of diet, it is possible, if the composition of the diet is known, to calculate the total intake. For the individual this is a simple but tedious exercise; but if it is desired to get a general figure for the population of a whole country or even for a smaller area, the task may be difficult and complex. With the aid of dietary surveys it is possible to make estimates of the average intake of fission products, but these dietary surveys are difficult to make, and the conclusions reached from their use require careful interpretation.

The estimation of radioactive nuclides in individual foods, even though it may be repeated at regular intervals in order to ascertain the way in which the contamination is changing, does not enable us to forecast future trends. Too many unknown factors are involved. We can reach a reasonably accurate estimate only if we have studied the movement of the radioactive nuclides in the food chain and determined the contamination at different stages.

Each of the three elements with which we are concerned, strontium, cesium, and iodine, behaves in a different way and must be considered separately in its passage through the food chain. There are, however, certain generalizations which can usefully be made.

Radioactive materials in the atmosphere can reach the earth's surface either by direct deposition or in rain, contaminating both bare soil and vegetation. Broadly speaking, the greater the rainfall the heavier is the rate of deposition, but there is no definite relationship between the two. Much depends on the form the rain takes and the type of cloud from which it falls. It is safe, however, to assume that areas with heavier rainfall will also have higher degrees of contamination.

The extent of deposition also varies with latitude. Due to

the pattern of testing and to meteorological factors, it is heavier in the northern hemisphere and appears to reach a maximum between 40° and 60°. Hence, it is in areas of high rainfall in this latitude that we must look for the highest levels of radioactive material in foodstuffs.

The material deposited on the leaves will be washed downward by successive rains. If the plant has deeply cupped leaves, this action of rain will serve only to concentrate the radioactive material in the axials. If the leaves do not retain water, the rain will carry the contaminated material into the root base and into the soil.

The movement of fall-out is not only downward; there is also a very considerable lateral movement due to wind in periods of drought and to run-off during heavy rains. In addition to these natural forms of redistribution, the farming activities of man and his domestic animals must be taken into account. The animal grazing contaminated herbage collects the fall-out remaining on or contained in the leaves over a wide area and concentrates it in its body tissues, in its milk, and in its excreta.

All these are local forms of redistribution, except where the run-off carries the fall-out down into a major river. They are primarily of importance in connection with the drawing of a representative sample of soil or growing plants and with the proper interpretation of the analytical data from animal products, particularly milk.

Man, by his distribution of food, transports fall-out over great distances. He harvests his food in one area and distributes it to many others, so where it is bought is no indication of its source. Therefore, while the analysis of purchased foods is essential in determining contamination in a diet, it is of little or no use as a means of studying the movement of fall-out in the food chain. Failure to appreciate this quite elementary point has led to some erroneous conclusions.

The radioactive substance falling on the leaves of a plant will be held there until it is washed or blown off, and if it is soluble, part will be absorbed.

The material which is not absorbed may, if the leaves are eaten by animals or man, enter the human diet. Cattle grazing the herbage will transfer a portion to their milk and hence to human food. Leaf vegetables and salads will add radioactive material to the diet unless it is removed in cooking or washing.

The radioactive substances absorbed in the leaves cannot be removed in preparation for the table and will form, with material entering the plant in other ways, the total contamination which cannot be separated from the food and must be consumed with it.

The inflorescences of plants can be contaminated in the same way as leaves, particularly if they are so shaped as to entrap the deposit falling on them. Unlike leaves, however, the time during which they can be contaminated is very short. This form of contamination is particularly important in grain, but the amount depends to a large extent on the rainfall during the time of inflorescence. If the contamination occurs when the crop is nearly mature it will be chiefly in the peripheral parts, and the amount contributed to human diet will depend on how far the outer layers of the grain are removed in milling.

The radioactive fall-out which misses the leaves or is washed down from them will reach next the plant base; that is, the surface roots, which are either above the soil level or only thinly covered with soil. The root systems of different plants vary greatly in character. In some there is little surface rooting while others, such as grasses in permanent pasture, have a thick mat of surface roots. These roots absorb plant nutrients, and any radioactive substances whose stable isotopes are normally taken up in the plant base will pass into the plant. This form of absorption is of great importance, in that the fall-out material is not diluted by elements with similar chemical characters occurring in soil in much greater quantities. The radioactive material which reaches the soil is held first by the soil particles in the upper layers from which the plants feed. Here it will be absorbed slowly in quantities dependent on stable elements with which it has to compete. At the same time it will be subject to leaching, which carries it down into the lower layers of soil where it is available only to the deepest rooted plants and hence is no longer a serious danger.

We have, therefore, direct absorption of radioactive material by the leaves and flowers of plants, indirect absorption from the soil, and a combination of direct and indirect absorption from the plant base, depending on how far this consists of soil-free root mat and how far of a loose root structure mixed with soil.

The foliar and floral and much of the plant base absorption must come from recently deposited radioactive material, since there can be no more than a temporary accumulation in these areas of the plant. The material taken up from the soil will, in contrast, consist in large part of older deposits which have been washed down from the bare soil surface, or from the plants growing on it, and stored in the soil.

If it can be shown that the fall-out which has been most recently deposited is the most important source of contamination, it follows that the uptake has been through the leaves, flowers, and root mat and that the annual, as distinct from the accumulated, deposit will largely control the level of radioactivity in food at any one time. The evidence that this is indeed the case in the years after nuclear test explosions, when the fall-out in the food chain is high, will be set out later in relation to the uptake of the different nuclides.

From the viewpoint of the danger from radioactive materials in the food, this immediate uptake by the plant is important. If all the fall-out passed directly into the soil and became incorporated as part of the available plant nutrients, it would be absorbed slowly and there would be a steady build-up in the soil. As a result, there would be a rise in the degree of contamination from year to year as the plant roots found more radioactive material available. With direct uptake by the plant, without pre-mixing with the soil, the amount absorbed will rise and fall with the annual deposit and there will be no steady increase due to accumulation of unabsorbed material.

Before the evidence for direct absorption by the plant had been obtained, it was assumed that the uptake was primarily from the soil and hence that it was closely related to the total fall-out from all atomic weapons tests. If this had been true there would have been serious cause for alarm, since the levels of radioactive material already found in foods would have been expected to rise each year as the total fall-out in the soil increased. The position in the late fifties was confused, because the steady increase in the annual rate of fall-out gave a rising level in plants, such as might have been expected by root absorption from an accumulation of radioactive material in the soil. Calculations based on this assumption suggested that if fall-out continued, the contamination of plants would reach dangerous proportions by the early sixties, if weapons testing continued to add each year more radioactive material so that there was an annual increase in the stored material in soil from which the plant could draw.

Analyses over the years have, however, shown this to be wrong. There is undoubtedly some uptake from the soil, but the values for contamination of crops have fluctuated with the annual rate of fall-out, showing that the major uptake is directly into the plant. It is reasonable, therefore, to conclude that unless there is a major increase in fall-out, the present levels in foodstuffs will not be materially exceeded, and if there is a reduction in annual fall-out due either to a cessation of testing or to "cleaner" bombs, the levels will quickly fall. Put shortly, relatively high levels in diet following past tests have been in the greater part linked to the current fall-out.

The uptake from the soil is controlled by many complex factors which tend to slow down the process of absorption and to render part of the radioactive material unavailable to plants. If the soil is undisturbed, as in permanent pasture, the radioactive material stays near the surface for a considerable period, the concentration falling off with depth. The rate at which it moves down the soil profile is governed by the character of the soil; in soils where there is a rapid movement of water it is carried down quickly to the lower soil horizons. Cultivations affect this movement; plowing mixes the soil and may bury a recent deposit up to a foot in depth and bring to the surface older deposits.

The physical state of the fall-out also affects its incorporation into the soil. If it is in an insoluble form, only a slow release into solution and then into the soil complex will occur. Once the radioactive material is in solution, it comes under the influence of the exchange reactions which govern the distribution of ions between the soil solution and the solid phase. These reactions are extremely complex and depend on such factors as the colloidal clay and humus particles in the soil, the acidity of the soil, and the total concentration of salts.

With these considerations in mind, we can now move on to consider the fate of the different radioactive nuclides in fall-out when they reach the earth's surface. The most important of these is strontium-90. From the viewpoint of danger to health, we can ignore strontium-89, as its short half-life of 53 days renders it relatively harmless. It is, however, valuable to know the ratio of strontium-90 to strontium-89. If we know the relative proportions of these isotopes reaching the earth, we can get a fair estimate from the change in this ratio of the time the material has been in the food chain. The lower the proportion of the short-lived isotope, the older is the material. If we know the ratios in precipitation and in plant material, we can determine how much has gone directly into the plant and how much has entered after being stored in the soil. It is by this means and by direct experiment that the high proportion of strontium-90 entering the plant by foliar, floral, and stem-base absorption was demonstrated.

The amount of strontium-90 deposited over relatively long

periods of time has been determined by the analysis of soils from undisturbed sites bare of vegetation, the amount deposited over short intervals by collecting precipitation and determining the strontium-90 present. Because of the great complexity of the methods required for the determination of strontium-90 in the presence of strontium-89 and other radioactive substances, the number of these estimations in precipitation and in soil, plants, and animals must be kept to a minimum and the samples must be bulked wherever possible. Moreover, the estimations, depending as they do on measuring the decay product yttrium, take several weeks to complete. The lay public is apt to call for more estimations and more rapid publication, without understanding either the difficulties involved or the errors which may arise from samples collected over too short a period. It is hardly necessary to say that to attempt a short cut by estimating the total radioactive strontium and deducing from this the amount of strontium-90 is highly dangerous. If the fall-out is of more recent origin than is assumed in such a deduction, the larger quantities of strontium-89 present may give what appears to be an alarmingly high result for strontium-90; if the material is older than is assumed, the relatively low content of strontium-89 will lead to a misleadingly low figure for strontium-90.

The behavior of strontium in the soil, in plants, and in animals is qualitatively similar to that of calcium. When plants are grown in simple inorganic solutions they take up calcium and strontium in the proportions in which these elements are present in the solution, so that the more calcium present for a given amount of strontium, the less strontium will find its way into the plant; in other words the calcium "dilutes" the strontium. It is convenient, in considering the relative movement of strontium and calcium at different points in the food chain and their final absorption by man, to speak in terms of the relationship of the ratio between strontium-90 and calcium in a sample and that in its precursor. The first of these ratios divided by the second gives us a third ratio, usually called the Strontium-90–Calcium Observed Ratio (O.R.). Thus, in the uptake of calcium and strontium by plants from inorganic solutions, as the ratio in the plant is the same as in the solution, the Strontium-90–Calcium Observed Ratio (O.R.) is 1. If the proportion of the calcium taken up had been more than that of strontium, the value for the O.R. would have been less than one.

As under normal growing conditions the calcium available to the plant greatly exceeds the stable isotope of strontium, the amount of the latter element taken up is always small. The absorption by the plant of the minute fraction of the total strontium which is radioactive is controlled in the same way by the quantity of calcium.

When strontium-90 first enters the soil it is in competition with smaller amounts of calcium than at greater depths. Shallow-rooted crops can then be expected to take up more of the radioactive material than those with deeper roots; this has been shown experimentally to be so.

All the calcium in the soil is not available to the plant, some being involved in complexes with which the plant roots cannot deal. The estimation, therefore, of the total calcium in a soil does not give us an indication of what the plant will absorb. By suitably extracting the soil, however, it is possible to determine the available calcium.

The ratio of strontium-90 to the calcium in the edible parts of a plant has been shown to be the same as the ratio of strontium-90 to the available calcium in the soil on which it is grown; that is, the O.R. is 1, as it is for plants growing in inorganic solutions.

With foliar and floral absorption there is no question of competing elements other than those present in the fall-out itself, which can be ignored. So long as fall-out containing strontium remains on the leaves or flowers it will be absorbed, to a degree depending on its solubility. This contamination must arise from material deposited during the growth of the leaf or inflorescence.

Strontium moves in only one direction in the plant, from the roots upward. Therefore, the strontium-90 absorbed in the leaves will remain there and will not be conveyed downward to other parts of the plant.

In annual plants, the root base absorption must also consist only of material deposited during the period of growth of the plant. In perennial plants, however, particularly those with prostrate stems, strontium-90 deposited in rolled leaf bases and surface roots at any time during the life of the plant may be held and accumulated until it is either washed down or absorbed by the plant.

Strontium-90 entering through the root base will pass up into the leaves and other parts of the plant without having to compete for entry with calcium as it does in the soil. By comparisons of the strontium-89 and strontium-90 in the inner leaves of such plants as cabbage, which are not exposed to direct contamination and which — because of the unilateral movement of strontium — cannot receive material absorbed by the outer leaves, it has been shown that the major part of radioactive strontium present is of recent origin, thus providing evidence of the extensive uptake of strontium through the root base. Further evidence of root base uptake can be obtained by protecting plants from all forms of strontium-90 contamination other than from the soil; this is found to vary between 0.2 and 2.0 per cent per year of the strontium-90 present in the soil. The total strontium-90 in the plant is much higher than can be accounted for by such a rate of uptake. The exact proportions of strontium-90 directly absorbed and obtained indirectly from the soil varies, however, according to the form and amount of the annual fall-out, the nature of the plant, and the stored material available in the soil.

It may at first sight appear alarming, when we consider the ingestion of plant material by man, that so much of the strontium-90 entering the plant does so undiluted with calcium. Fortunately, the method of entry of the strontium-90 has little effect on the final ratio of strontium-90 to calcium in the plant. Calcium drawn from the soil is always present in the plant in the same large quantities by whatever route the strontium-90 enters. The calcium status of the soil is, however, important since it materially influences the calcium content of plants grown on it. The higher this is in relation to the strontium-90 content, the less will be the danger to man eating the plant material or drinking milk from an animal that has eaten it.

When a man or animal eats plant material containing strontium and calcium, both elements are in part absorbed by the gastrointestinal tract. The part not absorbed is excreted in the feces. The amount entering the body will vary with the conditions, but it does not often exceed 20 per cent. With domestic animals, the dung is returned to the land. If it remains on or is added to pasture, some will be taken up by the pasture either through the leaves or through the plant base and reingested by the grazing animal. The rest will be washed down and slowly mixed with the soil, where it will accumulate and be taken up slowly by the pasture or other plants which may be grown in the field or it may be fixed in the soil so that it is no longer available. If it is spread on arable land it will be mixed with the soil at a considerable depth and reabsorbed only slowly by the crop grown on the land.

Although the animal body can use both calcium and strontium, there is a definite discrimination against strontium. The ratio of strontium to calcium resulting in the body is only about a quarter of that in the diet. Of the calcium and strontium absorbed, only a fraction is built into the bones and becomes a permanent danger, the rest being excreted. The amount of these elements fixed in this way depends on the age of the animal. In the young there is rapid bone growth in which the available calcium and strontium are used in roughly the ratio in which they are present in the body. If strontium-90 is present as part of the total strontium, it will be built in the bones in the same way, in proportion to the amount present. In the adult there is a turnover in the strontium-calcium content of only part of the bone, so that with a constant strontium-90–calcium ratio in the body, a steady state should be reached in which the strontium-90 content of bone becomes constant when that part of the bone which is affected reaches equilibrium with the plasma.

One other aspect of strontium-90 contamination remains to be considered; the amount secreted in milk. Here there is a further discrimination against strontium, the ratio of strontium-90 to calcium in milk being only one-tenth of that in the diet of the cow. The same ratio applies in woman, her milk containing one-tenth of the strontium-90 in her diet. A breast-fed baby will receive only one one-hundreth of the strontium-90 ingested by the cow whose milk the mother drinks, and only one-tenth of the strontium-90 in the rest of her diet.

We see, therefore, that strontium-90 enters the food chain through four routes of absorption by plants. In three of these, the foliar, floral, and plant base, the absorption is direct without previous dilution with calcium and is governed by the annual rate of fall-out. It is, however, diluted with calcium in the plant, to an extent dependent on the calcium uptake from the soil. The fourth route, through the roots of the plant, is from strontium-90 mixed with the soil, and in this instance it is diluted by the soil calcium and is only taken up in the same ratio to calcium as that existing between the available strontium and calcium in the soil.

Of the strontium in the diet, only about 20 per cent is absorbed in the intestine, and the ratio of strontium-90 to calcium is reduced to about one-quarter. This strontium-90 can enter bone along with calcium and does so in the ratio in which it is present in the body fluids. The amount going into bone depends on the rate of bone formation or, in the adult, on the extent of turnover. With a steady level of intake, the level of strontium-90 in bone should reach a steady state.

Before we go on to consider the total amounts of radioactive material in a composite diet, the movements of cesium-137 and iodine-131 must be examined.

Cesium, in contrast to strontium, is retained in the soil in a form in which it is not easily available to the plant. It therefore enters the food chain primarily by direct absorption by the plant. Unlike strontium, too, it moves freely in the plant so that it may be concentrated in root tubers such as potatoes.

The behavior of cesium is physiologically similar to that of potassium. It is efficiently absorbed by the gastrointestinal tract, it is secreted into milk, and it accumulates in the body cells. There is, however, not the same definite relationship between potassium and cesium that there is between calcium and strontium. The one major factor determining the effect of cesium-137 is its rapid turnover within the body. In all animals it is eliminated in a matter of days. Unless there is a very high level of continuous contamination, the effect of cesium-137, in spite of its long half-life, is small and it presents no danger comparable to that of strontium-90.

The half-life of iodine-131 is so short that only when high concentrations reach pasture on which cattle are grazing must it be seriously considered. About 5 to 10 per cent of the iodine-131 ingested by cattle appears in their milk. This iodine is concentrated in the thyroid glands of those consuming the milk. The published levels of iodine-131 derived from atomic explosions have never been high enough in the past to suggest danger comparable to that from strontium-90. Only in the accident at the Windscale reactor have the amounts been such as to warrant the withdrawal of milk for a short time. The deposit there was from a low level and was concentrated in a limited area, to give a concentration of iodine-131 on the pasture of an entirely different order from that occurring after nuclear test explosions.

We are left, therefore, with strontium-90 as the one really important potential long-term danger to health arising from fall-out. We have so far only considered its entry into the food chain through plants and animal products, but there is one other item of diet, namely, fish, which may contain strontium-90. The sea known to be the most heavily contaminated is the North Pacific. In Japan, sea-fish form a very important element in the diet, amounting to as much as 100 gm. per day. The inhabitants of Japan may, therefore, be accepted as the population receiving the largest amount of strontium-90 from seafood. Careful estimations have shown that this is very small, not more than 0.5 per cent of that coming into the diet from terrestial sources.

With some knowledge of the behavior of strontium-90 in the food chain, it is possible to proceed to the consideration of the amounts of this radioactive material in different diets arising from the contamination of plants, this being the only route of importance to man. We can also attempt some forecast of what will be the effect of different fall-out patterns arising from nuclear explosions.

As we have seen, there appears to be a fairly constant relationship between the strontium-calcium ratios in the diet and those in the body and in milk. It has also been shown that the strontium-calcium ratio predicted in the body from a knowledge of that in the diet gives a reasonable indication of the radioactive contamination of bone. The amount of radioactive strontium ingested is governed by the calcium intake; the more calcium there is in the diet for a given amount of strontium, the less strontium will be retained in the body.

The calcium content of the diet is, therefore, of equal importance to that of strontium-90. In order to estimate the amount of strontium-90 to which the body is exposed, it is essential to determine the ratio of strontium-90 to calcium in the total diet.

It is, however, no easy task to determine the strontium-90–calcium ratio in a diet. There are two ways in which this can be done: to collect samples of representative whole diets and determine the total calcium and strontium-90 in the diet, or to analyze the individual items of the diet and to build up from these the calcium–strontium-90 ratio in the complete diet. The first method has the serious disadvantage that the figures obtained can be used only for the particular diet selected. Any variation from this, as between different neighborhoods, different income levels, or different age groups within a community, can only be resolved by other analyses of complete diets. A change, too, in the source of any item in the diet may invalidate the result. It has, however, been used with some success in countries where there are large communities with a common diet derived from local produce.

The second method has many advantages. Once the values for individual items of diet are known, the values for different whole diets derived from them can be calculated. If any item is derived from a new source, it can be analyzed and the correction made to all the diets in which it is included. Great care, however, must be taken to make certain that the sample for each item is correctly drawn so that it is fully representative, not only of the area from which it comes but also of any variations in time. The value required in considering a diet is the average figure over a period of time. It is this that governs the accretion in bone, not any short-term abnormally high or low value. Unnecessary alarm has been caused by the publication of individual figures which were far above the average, suggesting a total intake of strontium-90 greatly in excess of what was in fact being built into bone.

Owing to the difficulty of estimating strontium-90, samples can, with advantage, be bulked. By drawing regular samples over a period and mixing them, it is possible to get from one analysis the average level of contamination. This has been done successfully with milk.

The samples must be drawn from as near the source as possible, in order to make certain of their true origin. It is of little value to buy samples at the point of consumption, because the source may change. This applies particularly to preserved foods sold in large centers of population.

Where a diet is complex there may be many items to consider, but it is necessary to consider only those which contribute major amounts of calcium, as strontium is always associated with these.

Thus, in the United Kingdom diet milk, cream, cheese, and flour contain 80 per cent of the strontium-90. If leaf and root vegetables are added, over 90 per cent is accounted for. If the strontium-90–calcium ratio is determined for these items of diet, it gives a sufficiently accurate estimate of the total contamination. In many Eastern countries the major contribution of strontium-90 comes from cereals; hence the calcium–strontium-90 ratio in these is of primary importance.

In order to obtain values for the contamination to which different population groups are exposed, it is necessary to ascertain their ordinary diet. This involves surveys, which must be carried out under very carefully controlled conditions. This, in itself, is a matter for careful study, and absorbs much skilled labor. Enough is, however, now known of the diets in different parts of the world and of the contamination of the different items, to assess the dangers arising from fall-out.

A careful analysis has been made by the United Nations' Food and Agricultural Organization of all available data; this is published under the title "Dietary Levels of Strontium 90 and Caesium 137." The conclusion reached is that in the period 1957–60 the diet of no population for which data were available reached one-tenth of the permissible level set by the International Commission on Radiological Protection, and that for most populations it was less than one-twentieth. Since the level of strontium-90 is primarily controlled by the annual fall-out, which has shown no major increase since that period, we can rest assured that we are not at present subjected to a dangerous level of radiation from fall-out. The annual rate would have to be increased roughly tenfold before there was need for alarm.

This does not mean that we should not strive in every way to keep this danger under control; if we can do so, we shall suffer no harm from what man has already done. The danger lies not in the past, where by good fortune nature has protected man from his own folly, but in the future, where the folly might be so great that the protective mechanism would be of no avail.

# COMMENTARY

## By C. L. COMAR

**S**IR WILLIAM has presented an authoritative and interpretative review of food chain matters. There is little that I would want to or could add. However, since a commentary is expected — perhaps a few words about some current problems from a more specific national viewpoint are in order.

First, where does the legal responsibility lie for protection of the public against food contamination by radioactivity? The situation is unclear almost to the point of chaos, but presently appears to be as follows: Contamination by debris from nuclear weapons tests is under no legal control, since events are determined by the governments of those countries in possession of nuclear weapon capabilities. The Atomic Energy Commission has responsibility only for proper usage of man-made radioactive materials and reactor operation. The Department of Health, Education, and Welfare has primary responsibility within the executive branch for the collation, analysis, and interpretation of data on environmental radiation levels. The Food and Drug Administration has responsibility for radioactive contaminants in food (other than meat and poultry) in interstate commerce, while the Department of Agriculture has responsibility for meat and poultry. From the practical standpoint, any regional action in regard to modification of food supplies and diets will have to be taken by state health agencies, calling upon national bodies for advice when desired; this is in the long-standing tradition of the Public Health Service. It offers the advantage of suiting action to local needs but also the possible disadvantage of confusion, with each state acting independently under different guidance.

To a group known as the Federal Radiation Council falls the crucial and most difficult task of setting radiation standards: that is, establishing levels of food contamination at which preventive or remedial action is recommended. This body, which was created in 1959, is composed of representatives from all the national agencies that have an interest in any aspect of radiation. Its major function is to advise the president with respect to radiation matters directly or indirectly affecting health, including guidance for all federal agencies in the formulation of radiation standards and in the establishment and execution of programs of co-operation with states.

Since there is presently a controversy about current $I^{131}$ levels in milk, the status of radiation standards is presented in terms of this radionuclide. In 1961 the Federal Radiation Council established guidelines for the intake of $I^{131}$. In brief, the Federal Radiation Council guidance for $I^{131}$ is represented by an annual averaged intake of 100 micromicrocuries per day or an annual intake of 36,500 micromicrocuries as the upper level of Range II, above which application of control measures is to be considered. Although the guidelines were originally presented with appropriate qualifications especially restricting their application to normal peacetime industrial operations, there seemed to be an understanding in the minds of most individuals that these standards should also apply to fall-out.

It must be emphasized that the Federal Radiation Council guidelines were not based on scientific evidence of the biological effects of radiation exposure. They were based on judgment involving comparison with natural background radiation, the expected benefits from the exposure, and the practicality of keeping exposures below the levels that were set. In the fall of 1962, concentrations in milk in some areas of the country approached the levels at which action appeared to be warranted by the Federal Radiation Council guidelines. As a matter of fact, at least one state undertook to reduce $I^{131}$ levels in commercial fresh milk by arranging for farmers to utilize stored feed instead of pasture for dairy herds. It requires little imagination to recognize the imponderables that must be balanced in arriving at such a decision.

In response to this situation, the Federal Radiation Council issued an official statement on September 17, 1962, which affords some clarification and from which the following excerpts are paraphrased:

1. The Federal Radiation Council does not recommend preventive measures under present circumstances.

2. Radiation exposures anywhere near the guides involve risks so slight that countermeasures may have a net adverse rather than favorable effect on the public well-being. The judgment as to when to take action and what kind of action to take to decrease exposure levels involves consideration of all factors.

This matter is now receiving consideration by the Federal Radiation Council, and it is expected that an official position will be developed shortly on guidelines for action that are applicable to fall-out contamination. It is unfortunate that some confusion and loss of public confidence have resulted from the setting of a protection standard which in the public mind has had to be revised under pressure of events. However, this is the inevitable result of the public health requirement for a single value to serve as an action point when in fact such a value cannot be established on the basis of present scientific knowledge and assessment of nationally variable factors.

A word now about personal anxiety: Should individuals be anxious about effects of fall-out from past tests on personal and family well-being? Compare the risk with that from automobiles: 40,000 fatalities a year on the highways; at the most, forty additional cases of cancer from tests through 1961. These figures are not quoted to justify any unnecessary addition to human suffering but simply to emphasize that we do not feel personal anxiety about this level of risk. A mother would be a thousand times more effective in preventing harm to her children by keeping them out of automobiles than by reducing their intake of radioactive material in food.

Although there need not be individual anxiety about fall-out, there must be concern and interest on the part of officials and scientists who have authorized responsibility. It is prudent that knowledge be obtained to cope with any foreseeable contingencies, and research must be done on preventive measures. The fact that such work is under way, however, should not be interpreted by the lay public to indicate that these measures are needed or desirable under existing conditions.

In general, a remedial measure to be useful must fulfill certain requirements: (1) It must be effective. (2) It must be safe: that is, the health risk from its use must be less than that from the radiocontaminant. (3) It must be practical from the standpoint of application. (4) Responsibility for application must be defined. (5) The impact on the public must be considered.

Specific comments are limited to $I^{131}$ since this radionuclide, if any, will probably be the first to require action. Remedial measures for $I^{131}$ are relatively simple because of its short half-life and because it reaches the public primarily in a single identifiable food, milk. Measures that have been proposed are listed as follows: (1) feeding of dairy cows with stored feed, (2) placing of young children and pregnant and lactating women on evaporated or powdered milk; (3) use of stored milk products (e.g., refrigerated, frozen, canned); (4) pooling of milk from regions of high contamination with that from regions of low contamination; and (5) addition of stable iodine to the diet.

Strontium-90 decontamination is a much more difficult problem and as yet there are no preventive measures that fulfill the criteria of effectiveness, safety, and feasibility. This is true despite research along such lines as soil control, liming of soils, removal from milk by ion exchange, or addition of stable calcium to dairy herd or human diets.

It is emphasized that the biological cost of past weapons tests of 150 to 200 megatons of fission is small enough that people will most likely do themselves a disservice if they take individual action to attempt a reduction in radiation exposure.